The Story
of the Old Testament

DAVID TALLEY

RECLAIMED
PUBLISHING

ISBN 13: 978-0615872544
ISBN 10: 0615872549

CONTENTS

FOREWORD

It is a joy to write this book. I have been in Christian ministry for over 30 years, and I have been a university professor for a majority of those years. As I reflected on my own personal journey, I realize that there are two primary reasons for writing this book.

First, when I was a first-year seminary student, I greatly admired my Hebrew Grammar professor, Dr. Richard Averbeck. What caught my attention was his obvious love for the Lord. I followed him wherever he went and took every course he offered because I wanted to love Jesus like he did. One day I was seated in his office, probably taking up far too much of his time with my endless questions, when I asked, "Why did you become a professor of Old Testament?" His answer was that, when he became a Christian, he realized that there was a void in the church's understanding of the Old Testament. As a result, he committed his life to helping the church understand the Old Testament better. Well, right there on the spot, unknown to him, I made that same commitment, and I have faithfully followed this commitment through the years. I love studying, teaching, and preaching the Old Testament and bringing people to a greater understanding of its message. And, as with this professor who impacted me so greatly, I have grown in my love for Jesus in the process.

Second, when I was a first-year professor putting together my course syllabus for Old Testament Survey, I began to reflect on teaching methodology, course assignments, and strategy for approaching such a vast amount of material. My reflection helped me to understand that the major weakness of my years of biblical/theological training was the lack of actual study of the biblical text. In my years of study, I read more books about the Bible than I actually read the Bible itself. So I determined to design my course in such a way that students would be required to engage the story of the Old Testament. I wanted them to read it with attentiveness. I wanted them to feel comfortable navigating the pages of the Old Testament. I wanted them to understand the basic flow of these 39 seemingly distant and complicated books. I wanted them to believe that the message of the Old

Testament mattered to their lives. I became passionate about these desires.

These concerns still guide my ministry in the classroom and my research interests. They are the reasons I set out to write this book. I desire to help the church understand the Old Testament better, and I want to get people into the biblical text. But still ... why write another book on the Old Testament, especially a survey book? This is a very important question. I have asked it over and over. Yet, as I use the survey resources that are available, I always find myself thinking that there is a better way to present the material of the Old Testament and to invite the reader into its riches. This book is an attempt to do just that.

An Overview

The overall goal of this book is to help the people of God grow in the grace and knowledge of the Lord Jesus Christ. The story of Jesus, the Messiah, begins in the Old Testament. This testament provides a necessary foundation for understanding the history of redemption. Many people in the church are afraid of the contents found in these pages, but I believe it is absolutely necessary for the church to engage this material.

This book is written to help the reader become a better student of the Old Testament. The first two chapters are introductory, yet they contain information important for reading this book and the Old Testament. Chapter One gives my rationale for why we study the Bible, namely the Old Testament. God has given us his word to help us grow in our relationship with the Lord and our ability to love. Chapter Two introduces the reader to the concept of THE STORY. I have found that this is the single most important tool for helping believers understand the Old Testament.

Chapters Three through Twenty-Five will alternate between content, theology, and special introductory material or topics necessary for understanding the Old Testament. The "content chapters" seek to help you understand the basics of each biblical book so that you can grasp the overall content. Most survey books are packed with abundant information about the individual books of the Old Testament, but I have sought to reduce the material to pertinent information, which I think is necessary for the average student of the Bible. I want the Old Testament books to be accessible, but not overwhelming.

The theology chapters are written to help you move beyond the content and actually engage the material in a manner that brings it into everyday life. I also want to make the material applicable: Why do we have these stories preserved for us? What do they have to do with our lives? My goal is to make it clear that "all scripture is inspired by God and *profitable*..." (2 Timothy 3:16-17). The Old Testament is rich and powerful. It is like a mirror into our own lives if and when we are able to engage the stories.

The other chapters, which are devoted to special introductory material or topics necessary for understanding the Old Testament, will hopefully assist you in grasping some larger or more focused issues in the Old Testament. My goal is that you have a stronger foundation from which to read its contents.

Appendix One is provided for those of you who want to go deeper in your study of the books of the Old Testament. I include this model for you to use as you desire—modify it, adapt it, and make it your own. I hope that it will help you know God intimately and let him change your heart and life through a deep engagement with the truth of his word.

The theology chapters include a "Making It Real" section at each chapter's close. These questions help you focus what you have read and bring it to bear upon your own life. My goal is for your life to be enriched as you think through the messages of each book. This goal is connected to Chapter One and why we study the Old Testament. It is to impact us. We are not disconnected from it. It is written to us and for us. We must learn to feed on it and grow by it.

I offer this book as an opportunity to help people in this endeavor. May God bless us all as we seek to know him better through his word. I do hope that this book helps you grow in your love for Jesus and in your desire to be a part of the story he continues to write until he returns. I pray that it brings you into a deeper relationship with Jesus Christ. May you find yourself loving Jesus more and more as you read the words he has preserved for you so that you can know him. To him be the glory forever and ever. Amen.

CHAPTER ONE:
WHY STUDY THE OLD TESTAMENT?

Why do we study the Old Testament? It is important to answer this question at the very beginning. If we cannot get the answer right, then the writing of this book may be futile.

Have you ever been lost? Of course you have. Everyone has had this experience at some point in life. It is a frustrating experience. So, throughout the history of humanity, maps have played an important role to keep us moving in the right direction. Today, GPS has become commonplace in people's lives. You can find them in the car, in backpacks, or packed away with the travel gear.

We also get lost in living. The Bible becomes our "GPS" for living. Jesus boldly proclaimed, "I am the way, the truth, and the life" (John 14:6). In response to the Law,

Moses stated, "For it is not an idle word for you, indeed, it is your life." (Deut. 32:47). Ultimately, the Bible offers the only divinely inspired and, therefore, reliable foundation and guide for life. The story of the wise man and the foolish man in Matthew 7:24-29 clearly makes this point. The one who builds his house on the word of God is likened to the man who built his house on the rock, which can withstand the storms of life. Psalm 1 drives this point home as well. The one who meditates on the word of God is likened to a tree planted by streams of water, which bears much fruit. The blessed man, the one who is like a luxuriant tree, is one who is immersed in the word of God. We need the word to guide us, much like a GPS, through life.

The Lord intends that we take the reading and study of his word seriously and that we keep the truths we learn central to the way we think about life and the way we respond to him. His word is "profitable for doctrine, reproof, correction, and instruction in righteousness" (2 Timothy 3:16-17). In other words, it tells us how to live ("doctrine"), how to know when we are not living for him ("reproof"), how to change our focus back to him and his purposes ("correction"), and how to continue in the way of faithful living ("instruction in righteousness"). It is important to note that, when Paul wrote these words to young Timothy, he was referencing the Bible of their day, which was basically the Old Testament. The Old Testament is "profitable" for all these benefits. I realize that there may be many "obstacles" in accessing the message of the Old Testament for the average reader, which seems to limit the benefit, but we will put those aside for the moment. It is my hope that the remaining chapters of this book will help us with those. For now, we must stick with the question: "Why study it?"

Our Purpose

The Bible focuses on certain truths that need to become evident in the way we live. Ultimately, it is not an informational book; it is a transformational book. In its entirety, the Bible intends to affect the way we relate to God and to others. Consider the following passages:

"The aim of our charge is love that issues from a pure heart and a good conscience and a sincere faith" (1 Timothy 1:5).

According to Paul, his goal in teaching was that people would love better. He does not provide the object of this love, simply that love is the goal. Paul wrote much of the New Testament on a wide variety of topics, but in the end his goal is stated clearly. It is love.

"...earnestly desire the higher gifts. And I will show you a still more excellent way...So now faith, hope and love abide, these three; but the greatest of these is love" (1 Corinthians 12:31-13:13).

In this passage, Paul emphasizes that love outweighs any knowledge, giftedness, or abilities anyone may possess. Love is the solid foundation on which life and service are built. Without it, whatever is built is of no value. By definition, if we do not love well, then we do not serve well, no matter how gifted we might be. Love is the foundation on which all else is built.

"Teacher, which is the great commandment in the Law?" And he said to him, "You shall love the Lord your God with all your heart and with all your soul and with all your mind. This is the great and first commandment. And a second is like it: You shall love your neighbor as yourself. On these two commandments depend all the Law and the Prophets" (Matthew 22:36-40).

When Jesus summarized the Law, he made it very clear that love is the ultimate priority. He makes the connection that, if one were to consider all the teachings of the Law and Prophets in the Old Testament, it would be summarized in one concept, love. This love was to affect the two primary relationships, humanity's relationship with God and with one another. In other words, the Lord's plan is to repair the relationships that were broken by the fall in Genesis 3. Concerning humanity's relationship with God, Adam and Eve ran and hid from God, reflecting the brokenness of that relationship; concerning the relationship with other people, the man and the woman sought to tear one another down in their attempt to preserve themselves. This is followed immediately by the murder of Abel by his brother, Cain. In short, the purpose of God's dealings with humanity and all the Old Testament's instruction is love.

> "A new commandment I give to you, that you love one another: just as I have loved you, you also are to love one another. By this all people will know that you are my disciples, if you have love for one another" (John 13:34-35).

Again, Jesus makes a bold point teaching that the distinguishing mark of the church, as well as its individual members, is love. It is not proper doctrinal beliefs, or amazing outreach programs, or large church buildings full of people. That which distinguishes the church is love—a love that is able to work through all the difficulties of living in a fallen world in a manner that maintains unity and seeks out the interests of others above one's self. This is what identifies a follower of Christ. Consistent with the other teachings in the New Testament on love, Jesus makes strong connections between one's love for him and one's obedience to his commands (cf. 14:21 and 15:10-13). Love is not a mushy feeling of "warm fuzzies." Jesus is speaking of a love that is defined by the character of God and the Law, which God lovingly provides. This is a love that is willing to lay down its life for the sake of another as taught in 1 John 3:14 and 16.

As we read and study the Old Testament, it should be affecting the ways we live, and ultimately, the ways we love. This is our purpose in engaging the biblical text. Our lives need to be transformed and healed from the effects of the fall, which has damaged our primary relationships with God and with one another. The separation the fall brings is reversed as the word of God transforms our hearts and minds, making us more like him. It moves us from selfish preoccupation to selfless preoccupation, leading us to offer others whatever is in their best interests—no matter what—to the glory of God. This is a true manifestation of love.

How do we study the Old Testament?

Even after we have answered the question of "why?",

we are still left with "how?" When they first came onto the market, I bought a new iPod touch. It was a loaded, top of the line, and quite an amazing multi-functional piece of technology. But there was one problem. I had no idea how to tap into all that incredible technology. My default mode is to run to my children, who have grown up with technology and therefore approach it intuitively, to enlist their assistance. However, I must learn to utilize the technological abilities that I hold in my hand or I will always be left with minimal ability to take advantage of its many wonders; I will remain paralyzed unless I develop the ability to access the "power" of the iPod that I hold in my hand. If I access that "power," it will open up many doors of possibility for using the technology.

The same is true of the Bible, including the Old Testament. If we do not learn to access the treasures of these 39 books, we will not be able to avail ourselves of the wonderful message contained in its pages. We will only minimally understand the necessary foundation it provides for accessing the message of the New Testament. It will remain a large book that we hold in our hands, yet we will not know how to access the incredible gifts it offers us.

The answer to the question of "how?" is partly methodological and partly informational. For a methodology, which might be helpful in engaging the material of the Old Testament, see Appendix One. This methodology is a tool that will require any person to spend time meditating on the stories and books. Through this meditation and analysis, one can learn much of what is needed to begin to grasp God's message to us.

We study the Old Testament because it is an important part of the transforming word of God. It is intended to impact us with its rich theology. Therefore, it becomes important to know as much as we can about how these 39 books fit together, how they are intended to instruct us, and how they connect to our lives, as well as the individual messages of each book. This is the informational part of the "how?" question. We will explore this basic foundation in the next chapter.

CHAPTER TWO:
THE STORY OF THE OLD TESTAMENT

To navigate through the tedious, and often confusing, material of the Old Testament, one must have a strategy and a framework. The single most important lecture I give each semester to my students in my introductory survey course concerns the material in this chapter.

What are the major reasons the Old Testament is difficult to engage and understand? Students offer many reasons: difficulty in understanding the various laws, a different culture which seems distant and inaccessible, repetitious material with no obvious reason for the repetition, the apparent disconnect between Israel's history and our lives in the contemporary church, the chasm of time that separates us from the story and the resulting differences in our cultures, and the many odd practices such as sacrifice. Those who have sought to seriously engage the Old Testament have likely experienced many difficulties understanding its message. However, with a little insight into the manner in which these books are interconnected, it is possible to overcome some of these difficulties rather easily and immediately begin to access this information. The Old Testament contains over two-thirds of the revelation we have received from God, so it is imperative that we find ways to engage and understand this important message. God has given it to us so that we might understand him and the work he is doing in this world.

Have you ever thought about "the story" of the Old Testament? Have you ever sat and considered how to connect the dots of what often feels like disconnected and random information? Understanding the answers to these kinds of questions is a necessary first step for any person who wants to understand the Old Testament. If this desire exists, then there is good news for those who are interested! The Old Testament contains a clear, continuous narrative, or what we will call "THE STORY" throughout this book. If you can locate THE STORY, you will find a novel, and it is fascinating. Can you find this novel?

If you tried to create your own list, you probably encountered a lot of frustration. This is no easy task. On one level, it is difficult for us to think in terms of any book in the word of God as being less than central to what God wants to communicate. Let me emphasize that this assignment is not trying to communicate that certain parts of God's word are of lesser importance. Each book is essential for us to know, understand, love, and obey God, but each book also serves a certain purpose. The purpose of each book needs to be understood so that we can better understand what God is seeking to communicate. On another level, it is possible that we lack the understanding of each book that the above assignment requires. Furthermore, we may even have certain emotional connections with some books, which lead us to assume that these must be central to the narrative of the Old Testament. In light of these issues, is it possible to develop such a list?

How would you reduce the Old Testament in order to focus on the continuous narrative? It would be fun to interact with your thoughts. People, in general, like to include books they hear about most frequently like Isaiah with all of its rich Messianic prophecies, or books with an obvious story like Jonah, or familiar books like the Psalms. But actually none of these books are part of that continuous narrative that contains THE STORY of the Old Testament. When we survey the contents of the books of the Old Testament, we find that nearly all of the continuous narrative, which makes up THE STORY, is found in 11 books. In other words, if you were to read these eleven books in succession, you would basically read the essence of THE STORY of the Old Testament in its entirety. There is a beginning and an end. There is continuity. There is an identifiable story.

By considering the Old Testament in this manner, THE STORY becomes more accessible. However, if THE STORY is contained in only eleven books, then we must ask: "Are the other books unnecessary?" Or "What is the purpose of the remaining books?" Once we identify the 11 books, we must then demonstrate how the remaining 28 books fit into the narrative. THE STORY provides a structure for understanding each additional book's contribution to this story. By having such a framework, students of the Old Testament are equipped to navigate through the many oddities of the 39 books without losing their way. So which 11 books contain THE STORY?

The majority of THE STORY of the Old Testament is found in the following books: Genesis, Exodus, Numbers, Joshua, Judges, 1 Samuel, 2 Samuel, 1 Kings, 2 Kings, Ezra, and Nehemiah. If you were to read these eleven books in succession, beginning with Genesis and ending with Nehemiah, you would read through almost the entire story of the Old Testament. The reason it must be stated that it is "almost the entire story" is because there are some additional stories isolated in parts of other books. To keep it simple, we will only consider these 11 books. How is the continuous narrative found in these books?

Genesis begins THE STORY. The first 11 chapters introduce the narrative of the world's beginning and quickly cover 20+ generations of people, moving the story to Abram (Abraham). Then, THE STORY slows down and the next 39 chapters focus on just four generations of people: Abraham, Isaac, Jacob, and Joseph. The purpose is to detail the nation of Israel's beginning and show how they wound up as slaves in Egypt, awaiting the redemption of the Lord.

Exodus picks up THE STORY with Joseph's death. From there the narrative recounts the nation's hardships in Egypt prior to God's miraculous judgment against Egypt and redemption of Israel in the ensuing exodus from Egypt to Mt. Sinai. God then initiates his covenant with Israel and details the building of the Tabernacle so he can dwell in their midst. The focus of Exodus is on the life of Moses and his role in God's plan to grow Jacob's family into a nation with whom he makes another covenant. All this is preparation for taking the nation to the Promised Land.

Numbers continues THE STORY as Israel prepares to take the land. Again, the events occur in Moses' generation. After completing the Tabernacle, the nation organizes and then departs from Mt. Sinai. Subsequently, the first generation refuses to take the land, which results in God's judgment: 40 years of wilderness wanderings (which are also found in this book, though not in much detail). We do not have much information about this 40-year period because the focus of the book is on getting the nation to the border of the Promised Land, which is where Numbers closes.

THE STORY continues in the book of Joshua with Moses' death and the transfer of leadership to Joshua. He is entrusted with the task of bringing the people into the Promised Land. The narrative focuses on the conquest, division, and initial settling of the land of Canaan during the life of Joshua.

Joshua's death is described at the book's conclusion and reiterated at the beginning of the book of Judges where THE STORY continues. Since the land has already been settled, this book provides a glimpse of the nation's early years in the land when they were governed by judges. Each generation during this period experienced pieces of a simple, yet disturbing cycle: rebellion, judgment, crying out to the Lord, the Lord raising up a deliverer, deliverance, and a return to obedience for a time until the cycle repeats. Consequently, many generations are covered as the author seeks to show what this was like for Israel. When they are disobedient, there are consequences, but when they walk in faithfulness, the Lord in his mercy restores them to a place of blessing.

The era of the judges continues in the books of Samuel. Samuel is a judge, but his books move THE STORY from the period of the judges to the period of the kingdom. These two books include the transition from Samuel's leadership as the last judge to the king's leadership—beginning under King Saul and established under King David.

The books of Kings naturally flow from the books of Samuel, especially as they overlap at the end of King David's life. The books of Kings begin with David's latter years before detailing the transfer of leadership to Solomon as the new king and the story of King David's death. After King Solomon's unfaithfulness and the subsequent division of the kingdom, the remaining pages summarize the lives of the kings of the divided kingdom (northern kingdom of Israel and southern kingdom of Judah) and the solitary kingdom (southern kingdom of Judah alone). In these books the focus of THE STORY is the glory of the kingdom under Solomon's leadership, its tragic division, and the subsequent exile of both kingdoms, which seems to be the end of the nation as a whole.

The exilic period is crucial to the growth and formation of the nation. Since the land is the focus in the

Old Testament, in many ways and for our purposes, THE STORY takes a 70-year hiatus. But God is not done with his people. His story continues. The books of Ezra and Nehemiah tell the wonderful story of the people's return to the land. After the 70 years of exile are complete, these two books record three returns to the land under the leadership of Zerrubabel (to rebuild the Temple), Ezra, and Nehemiah (to rebuild the walls of Jerusalem) all of which are preparation for the coming Messiah and the restoration of the kingdom. God is continuing his work.

Note that THE STORY of the Old Testament ends with the book of Nehemiah. Yes, Nehemiah. It is not that God is done with his people. It is just that God will resume his story with the coming of the Messiah, which occurs in the New Testament gospels. The Old Testament story ends with anticipation as we look forward to the good news of the coming Messiah. The prophets build our anticipation as they fill in some details about what God is going to do and when he is going to do it. The Old Testament is actually the "first testament" or the prelude to the New Testament. Both contain God's story.

As you can see, there is a natural progression from book to book. Notice also the inclusion of the exile. This refers to the southern kingdom of Judah's exile, in which God's people are actually removed from the land and THE STORY is taken captive in Babylon for seventy years.

Books such as Daniel and Jeremiah provide some of the details of THE STORY for these years, but that is not the focus of our study. Our concern is God's work with his people in his land. Thus, we will focus on the movement of THE STORY from 2 Kings to Ezra and then explain how and why the exile is important.

Now that we have established that these 11 books set forth the continuous narrative of the Old Testament, let us turn our attention to how the remaining 28 books fit into THE STORY and the unique contribution each book makes. How do these six historic books, five poetic books, and seventeen prophetic books fit into the narrative? Are they necessary or do they just confuse THE STORY? Should they be excluded from the Bible altogether? I hope it is obvious that I do not believe these books are unnecessary, nor do I advocate removing them from our Bibles. They are integral to THE STORY, but they do not advance the actual overall sequence of THE STORY. These books are not extras. They play a vital role in the larger story, but how are we to understand them?

Leviticus does not advance THE STORY, but it does contain essential information for the nation. It fits within the one month gap separating the events of Numbers and Exodus (Exodus 40:17 and Numbers 1:1). The Tabernacle has already been built, but instructions for its proper use must be understood before Israel embarks on her journey to the Promised Land and the book of Leviticus provides them. It can be considered an addendum to the book of Exodus, serving as an instruction manual for the Tabernacle.

Deuteronomy does not advance THE STORY, but its position in the Pentateuch is important for the nation. It serves as a bridge between Numbers and Joshua. The book of Numbers ends with the nation on the plains of Moab and leadership being transferred to Joshua as the first generation, including Moses, must die before the people can enter the Promised Land. The second generation needs to be reminded of all the things that God has done for his people and the book of Deuteronomy provides three sermons by Moses which do that before he dies.

Ruth 1:1 states that the events of this book take place during the time period of the judges, so it fits within that narrative. It does not advance THE STORY, but it fits into THE STORY already told in Judges. It provides a contrast to the depravity of the book of Judges and shows that Godly people did exist during that time; a faithful remnant did exercise the kind of faith necessary to follow God in obedience. The book also shows that God is moving forward his plans for the Messiah as the seed of the one who is coming is preserved in a miraculous manner. Nothing and no one can stop the God's plan.

1 and 2 Chronicles repackage the events of Samuel

and Kings in order to encourage the people returning to the land after the exile. It demonstrates God's faithfulness in bringing his blessing and offers hope that if they are faithful in seeking the Lord, he will turn their situation around for good. There is an overlap in material but not in audience or purpose.

Esther does not advance THE STORY. This book occurs in conjunction with the events of Nehemiah, only in a different location. The people have returned to the Promised Land (as found in Ezra and Nehemiah), but this book shows that the Lord is watching over those who remain in Babylon. He is a good God who protects his own when they seek him regardless of where they are located. This serves as a powerful encouragement to the nation.

Job probably fits in the time of the patriarchs (this is the word used to identify Abraham, Isaac, Jacob, and Joseph) in Genesis. Many of the Psalms fit into the life of King David. King Solomon penned much of Proverbs, so they fit into his life and reflect his wisdom; he also authored Song of Songs and Ecclesiastes. Overall, the poetic books reflect the concerns, struggles, and emotions of those who walk daily in a covenant relationship with the Lord. They deal with various difficulties, such as suffering or the prosperity of the wicked, and can be studied as a unit because their focus is the same, but they do not advance THE STORY because they fit within THE

STORY of the 11 books.

The prophetic books can also be summarized as a unit. They do not advance THE STORY but rather fit in the time of the kingdom, specifically 2 Kings through Nehemiah. Each prophecy has a specific audience and a clear message. God is pursuing his people and letting the nations know that he is the ultimate authority in this world. The background for these prophecies can often be found in the narrative of the book where its prophecy fits. However, there are prophecies for which the exact context is unknown. These books also can be studied as a unit because their focus is the same; once one knows how the prophetic books "work," each book can be understood in a similar sense. Only the particulars of the specific message need to be studied.

Every book is an important revelation from God, but it helps us to know how the books fit together so we can follow the larger story of God's work in this world. Each book contributes individually to our overall understanding, but there is a very clear novel in THE STORY in the eleven books. It is a novel that draws us into what God is doing in this world to redeem people who have stubbornly rebelled against him. When we read THE STORY, the rebellion of humanity should disturb us, the mercy of God move us to tears, God's relentless pursuit of his people should awaken the wonder of the gospel, as the

Old Testament becomes a mirror to our own experiences. It is a powerful message indeed when we see ourselves in the story and in it meet the God whose love and mercy is overwhelmingly offered to those who humble themselves under the shadow of his throne.

This is the big picture. Hopefully it helps you to better understand how the Old Testament works. But as helpful as this framework might be, there is more to learn. Each book works powerfully in our own transformation when we understand the contribution it makes to the larger story, which God is inviting us to join.

CHAPTER THREE:
INTRO TO THE PENTATEUCH

The first five books of the Old Testament are referred to as the Pentateuch, which literally means "five-volumed." The books are identified as a unit because they share Mosaic authorship and continue one narrative. These books are also called the Law in the New Testament (cf. Luke 24:44) or the Torah in the Jewish tradition. These books focus on Moses and his role in bringing Israel to the plains of Moab before his death. Various parts of the Pentateuch are clearly ascribed to Moses (cf. Exodus 17:14; 34:27; Numbers 33:2; Deuteronomy 31:9, 24) so it becomes natural to view Moses as the author of the whole. Though this is widely debated in more liberal scholarship and must be taken into consideration, it is not of concern here.[1]

Neither Genesis, nor any of the books of the Pentateuch were meant to be read separately. They are each part of a larger volume telling one continuous narrative that begins with Genesis and is not completed until the last word of Deuteronomy. These five books are part of one large story. However, in keeping with our focus on THE STORY of the Old Testament, it is the books of Genesis, Exodus, and Numbers that carry forth THE STORY of God's work as found in the Pentateuch.

What a God! What a plan!

---

[1] This debate formulated in the "Documentary Hypothesis" or the "JEDP Theory." This theory would deny Mosaic authorship, setting forth a multiple authorship proposal. With this theory, the assumption is that the writing of the books occurred later than the life of Moses, even after the time of the exile. There were four authors: "J," the Yahwist, who wrote during the southern kingdom in 950 BC; "E," the Elohist, who wrote in the northern kingdom in 850 BC; "D," the Deuteronomist, who wrote in 650 BC (pre-Josiah); and "P," the priestly code, who composed ancient Mosaic traditions after the exile in 525 BC.

CHAPTER FOUR:
GENESIS

Genesis is an incredible book, which is full of drama. It begins the Bible, the Old Testament, and the Pentateuch. It focuses on both the grandest and most sobering themes of the Bible as the narrative invites readers to walk into people's lives and experience the messiness of their existence. It is a fast-moving narrative, which covers many years, yet provides only a few details of a few events. But most importantly, it is a book that matters to our everyday lives in the 21st century.

The title of this book in the English Bible originates from the one used in the Greek translation. Genesis means "origin," which is a reference to the many origins found in the book: the world, the human race, sin, the nations, and the Jewish people. The title in the Hebrew Bible is actually the first word in the book, which means "In the Beginning."

Major Divisions

The author organizes his narrative by use of the Hebrew word, toledoth, which is translated either as "this is the genealogy of," "this is the story of," or "this is the history of," depending on the context. The toledoth introduces new sections in the narrative as seen in: 2:4; 5:1; 6:9; 10:1; 11:10; 11:27; 25:12; 25:19; 36:1; 36:9; and 37:2. Generally, the beginning of the book, 1:1 – 2:3, is understood to be the introduction to Genesis from which the remainder of the toledoth passages flow. These toledoths were probably independent accounts or stories that were compiled into this book with the intent of providing the background for Israel's slavery in Egypt (see Exodus 1).

The toledoth introduces three types of material (see table on next page): vertical or "linear" genealogies, horizontal or "segmented" genealogies, and narrative material. Vertical genealogies play an important role in demonstrating the continuation of the "seed" from Adam to Abraham (i.e., ultimately leading to Messiah). They also serve to advance the story of Genesis to the next narrative focus. Horizontal genealogies are the least important, but this does not mean that they are insignificant; they are simply not important for our purposes. These genealogies basically show how certain families "spread out" and do not carry on the promise of the "seed" (cf. Genesis 3:15). The third type of toledoth, narrative material, introduces exactly that, narrative material.

Once the toledoths are isolated, the narrative becomes clear. As a result, we find five major narrative blocks in the book. Each of these blocks advances the narrative of Genesis and answers the book's questions. The major stories are:

1) The Creation and Degeneration of Society (2:4 – 4:26)

2) The Destruction of Humans/Society (6:9 – 9:29)

3) The Story of Abraham/Isaac (11:27 – 25:11)

4) The Story of Isaac/Jacob (25:19 – 35:29)

5) The Story of Jacob/Joseph (37:2 – 50:26)

These stories will be discussed in more detail below.

Although Genesis may be one of the longest books in the Bible with its 50 chapters, it is helpful to understand that the narrative can be reduced to these five powerful stories which point to the book's three major sections:

*1-2   The Creation of the World and Humanity (1)

*3-11   The Degeneration of Humanity (2)

*12-50   The Beginning of God's Plans to Redeem a People for Himself (3-5)

Combining stories 3-5 emphasizes the beautiful plan God is initiating to draw people into relationship with himself. It is only the beginning, but God will continue to move forward his plan until he brings it to fulfillment.

To simplify Genesis even more, chapters 1 – 11 are focused on universal concerns, including the origin of the world and the nations. These 11 chapters contain at least 20 generations of people, so the story moves fast and is full of gaps. Chapters 12 – 50 are focused on Israelite concerns. These chapters focus on only four generations (Abraham, Isaac, Jacob, and Joseph), so the story really slows down at this point. Clearly, this is where the author intended to get the reader. After describing how the world became evil, the narrative is ultimately focused on the story of Israel and the purposes of God to redeem humanity through his chosen people. This redemption is only in the initial stages, but God is on the move.

Main Message

The message of Genesis can be summed up in the word, "beginnings." Just about everything that is mentioned is a "first" or a "beginning." In this book we find the first people, the first day, the first night, the first sin, the first judgment, the first flood, the first sacrifice, and so on. All of these "firsts" serve as a foundation for understanding the Old Testament, the Bible, and even life itself. There is simply a lot of information that must be provided to give perspective to the entirety of the Biblical message. The book answers the questions:

Where did the world come from?

How did it get so messed up?

Is there any hope?

Where did God's people come from?

To answer these questions, the narrative includes the creation of the world and humanity, the degeneration of humanity, and the beginning of God's plan to redeem a people for his glory. When the book is read in light of these questions, which should spring from our own lives as well, it becomes a fascinating read.

Perhaps the most obvious feature of this book is the vast amount of time it covers. It includes at least 24 generations in its 50 chapters. And, remember, these generations are not your average "four score and seven years." The earliest people lived a long time, reaching almost 1,000 years old. The first 11 chapters cover at least 20 generations as evidenced by the genealogies in chapters 5 and 11, where each chapter contains 10 generations.[2] These genealogies fast forward the story to get to the next important event because the ultimate focus is theological, not informational. The author only communicates what he needs to communicate in order to make his point. The main purpose of these first 11 chapters is to provide the foundation for understanding human experience in this world. The focus is on basic information: creation, degeneration, and the beginnings of the movement of God to redeem. All the reader receives is a snapshot, nothing more. As a result, it leaves us with many unanswered questions, but God in his sovereignty has provided us everything necessary in order for us to know him, his purposes, and his work in this world.

In chapters 12 – 50, the narrative slows down to cover the four generations of the "patriarchs" or the early fathers of Israel: Abraham, Isaac, Jacob, and Joseph. The main purpose of these chapters is to provide the foundation for understanding the possibility of relationship with God. We are invited into the lives of these four patriarchs and are able to witness God's miraculous work in preserving them, extending them undeserved grace, and slowly advancing his plans to

---

[2] Each of these genealogies could exceed 10 generations as the use of exactly 10 generations could be attributed to a memory device rather than an exact accounting of the number of generations.

redeem a people for himself.

One must keep in mind when reading Genesis that the narrative begins with creation most conservatively in 4000 BC (as one possibility) and ends with the family of Jacob going down to Egypt in 1700 BC, covering at least 2300 years in a mere 50 chapters. This narrative is both powerful and foundational for the Old Testament books that follow. To summarize, chapters 1-11 provide a foundation for understanding human experience, and chapters 12-50 provide the foundation for understanding the possibility of relationship with God.

Now, let's look more closely at this book's contents.

INTRODUCTION

The five major narrative blocks discussed previously are preceded by the account of the creation of the world, which serves as an introduction to the toledoths which follow it. Creation is where everything begins. The familiarity of this story has truly become an obstacle for believers engaging the beauty of what is being described. The failure to read this story as it is written is an obstacle as well. The story is a poetic but true account of what happened. Regardless of how it is interpreted, one must not lose sight of God's power in this spectacular event. God spoke, and whatever he spoke came into existence...out of nothing. God is and has always been, and there is nothing else in existence outside of his creating it and bringing it into existence. One must not lose the incredible realities of this story.

STORY #1

The account of the creation of the world is followed by the story of the creation and fall (into sin) of Adam and Eve, which is one of the most familiar stories in the Bible. American culture still has an understanding of what is being communicated by a picture or a commercial with two naked people covered by fig leaves standing beside a fruit tree. Terms such as "forbidden fruit" are used because there is usually an image of what this means in the minds of many people. God created the world to be inhabited by people, so he created the man and the woman and put them into a garden, but humanity messed up the beauty of creation rather quickly.

Because of a faulty view of this story, God is often viewed as a demanding God, who seeks to exercise his control over this world and get his way in all things. However, a careful reading of this story shows a pattern that can be seen throughout the Bible: God's law, what he requires, is always preceded by his blessing. Before God puts any requirements on his people, he blesses them. Just read the description of the world he creates in chapter one. Wow! Then, read the description of the garden he makes specifically for humanity. Wow! God blesses over and over. He is a good God who seeks the good of the people he creates. Then, and only then, does he make demands of humanity—demands that are always for the good of his creation.

This is why what follows in chapters 3-4 is such a shocking story. Instead of resting in the goodness of this God who created them, humanity rebels against his goodness and consequences follow. These consequences still impact us today as we will see in the next chapter. However, even the consequences God imposes on humanity are for their good. Through these imposed consequences God is seeking to use difficulty to turn the hearts of his creation back to him so they can once again know his goodness. Read the story closely. God is not a malevolent dictator. God is kind and good and continues to seek the good of his creation.

STORY #2

As we move into the second story, we read that humanity's rebellion has progressed to the point that God looks down and sees only evil. Genesis 6:1-3 demonstrates that things have become so bad that God is sad over his creation and chooses to destroy the world he created. However, God preserves a remnant in Noah. Throughout the Old Testament we see that a faithful "remnant" is regularly preserved. God has a plan; he is moving it forward. Humanity will not stop its progress, and God will not completely give up on them.

Genesis 1-11 introduces us to the growing problem of sin in the world. What God created has truly been messed up. Each story builds in intensity and brings an understanding that, if left alone, the problem of sin will be the end of humanity. But God has an answer that he begins to provide with Story #3, which begins at the end of Genesis 11. He is an amazing and gracious God.

STORY #3

In this story we discover the first glimmers of God's plan. He has an answer. He has a solution. Evil continues, but God sets his affection on a person, the one through whom he is going to do a work for his glory: Abraham. God enters into a covenant relationship with him (Genesis 12, 15, and 17). In every covenant there are promises (the benefits of being in the covenant) and obligations (the responsibilities for being in the covenant). In this covenant, the Abrahamic Covenant, the obligations are faith (Genesis 17:1) and circumcision (Genesis 17:9-14). The promises are land (Genesis 13:14-17; 15:18-21; 17:8), seed (Genesis 12:2; 13:16; 15:1-6; 17:5-8), and blessing (Genesis 12:2-3). It is a personal covenant, given to a man and his family, and it serves as the foundation of God's covenant program with humanity, the way in which he is going to bring about reconciliation.

In this and each additional covenant, God reveals himself so that people can know him. This pattern of revelation eventually leads to the coming of the Messiah, the revelation of God in the flesh. These covenants culminate in the sacrifice of Jesus on the cross, bringing atonement to all who put their faith in him and him alone for salvation. Reconciliation. God is so good and merciful to offer such a plan.

This covenant is carried forward in the next two stories, anticipating the next revelation of God through a covenant with Israel in the book of Exodus.

STORY #4 AND STORY #5

The main point of these stories is that God is moving forward his redemptive plan. The covenant is being passed on to future generations. Abraham dies, but God is still very much alive and carrying out his plans in this world. Consistent with the Bible, we find that God is in no hurry to accomplish his purposes; he moves his plans forward at his pace. The covenant promises are extended to Abraham's son, Isaac. And, then, they are extended to Isaac's son, Jacob. Jacob is renamed Israel, and his twelve sons eventually make up the twelve tribes of the nation of Israel.

In Story #5 Jacob and his 12 sons are in Egypt. God brought this family there in order to take care of them. He prospers them and blesses them. And this story ends with Joseph's death. All of this is preparation for the wonderful things that God is going to do in the book of Exodus.

Context in THE STORY

The Genesis narrative introduces THE STORY found in the Old Testament, so it seeks to establish a foundation for understanding all that follows. It is written for the nation of Israel at Mt. Sinai, so it seeks to answer questions such as "How did we get here?" "Why is life so 'messy'?" "Who is God?" and "Who is Israel?"

Genesis ends with the account of Israel, in the family of Jacob, going down to Egypt (cf. Genesis 46-47; especially 46:8-27) and with Joseph's death (cf. 50:22-26). The book of Exodus begins with these same two stories in summary form (Israel going down to Egypt, Exodus 1:1-5, and Joseph's death, Exodus 1:6). This overlap creates a strong connection between the two books and demonstrates that Exodus is picking up THE STORY where Genesis ends. Before we pick up THE STORY in Exodus, we will explore the meaning of Genesis for our lives.

Looking Forward to Jesus

It is important in this study of the Old Testament to pause after each book and consider the question, "Where is Jesus?" The unfolding plan of redemption begins in the book of Genesis. Even though it will be many years before the Messiah comes, THE STORY constantly points to him. First, in Genesis 3:15, we find what many scholars call the "first gospel," in the words, "I will put enmity between you and woman, and between your offspring and her offspring; he shall bruise your head, and you shall bruise his heel." This prophecy contrasts the impact of the two seeds: the seed of the serpent who bruises the heel and the seed of the woman who crushes the head. The "seed of the serpent" is understood to be Satan (note the use of "you will bruise" in addressing the serpent) and all who follow him in seeking to destroy the name, person, and work of the Lord. All such attempts will only have a "bruising" effect. However, the eventual seed of the woman, the Messiah (note the use of "he will crush" in addressing the woman), will have a "crushing" effect. In other words, Satan will be effective in standing against the Lord throughout the years and even gain a following, but one day, namely at the death of the Messiah, he will be dealt a death blow and crushed, ultimately resulting in his eternal death in the Lake of Fire. The genealogies of the Old Testament are often concerned with the forward movement of this "seed."

Second, God makes a covenant with humanity. In Genesis we see the first covenant, the Abrahamic Covenant. God is making a way for sinful humanity to be in relationship with him. Ultimately, the only way this will happen is through Jesus, but in Genesis the possibility of relationship is a wonderful first step. The promises of this covenant with Abraham will be most fully and ultimately realized in the person of Christ (Galatians 3:16). He is "the seed," and he is the one through whom all the nations of the world will be blessed. "The land" is simply a precursor to a better land, the heavenly city and our eternal home, which is being prepared by Jesus (John 14:1-3).

Finally, Genesis 49:10 states, "The scepter shall not depart from Judah, nor the ruler's staff from between his feet, until tribute comes to him (or: "until Shiloh comes"); and to him shall be the obedience of the peoples." This verse brings a more extensive explanation concerning the Abrahamic blessing coming to the Gentiles. It will be through Judah, who is given royal status, and it will be fulfilled in the Davidic line, ultimately in the Messiah. All the peoples will be obedient to him and bring tribute to him in the end when every knee bows and every tongue confesses that Jesus is Lord.

The plan is vague in most respects and is only in its beginning, but God is making a way.

CHAPTER FIVE:
THEOLOGY OF GENESIS

Genesis should matter to us because it speaks into our lives. As was stated previously, the message of THE STORY is not merely informational, it is intended to be transformational. It is theology for living. In seeking to understand the theology of this book and why it matters to us, initially, we will focus on two major points: life as God intended it to be and life as we know it. The contrast between these will cause us to think in new ways about this narrative and hopefully draw us into a deeper relationship with our heavenly Father. Finally, we will make a point of application and consider how we are to respond to this life as we know it.

Life as God Intended It to Be

God had a clear plan when he created humanity. This plan was violated by the introduction of sin, but sin did not thwart God's ultimate plan for his creation. The message of the Bible clearly articulates that God's purpose for his creation is continuous throughout history—he is committed to bringing glory to himself by bringing humanity back into relationship with him. One way we can see this is by looking closely at the first two chapters of Genesis and comparing them to the last two chapters of Revelation. We will look at the parallels in a moment, but for now I simply want to point out that their primary emphasis is that God intends for his created beings to live in a paradise, which is not the present situation of our world.

The first two chapters of Genesis are often read and understood in a manner that is divorced from its intended context. As was discussed earlier, these chapters are part of the larger context of the Pentateuch, written by Moses to the nation as they wandered through the wilderness awaiting their entrance into the land that was promised to their forefathers over 400 years earlier. Consequently, the chapters are intended to bring perspective to that generation of Israelites by providing them a glimpse of God's magnificent plan to redeem his people from the painful consequences of sin. These chapters seek to answer questions like: How did we get here? Why is life like this? Does the Lord care about us?

Similar questions have been asked throughout history. The problem of evil and consequent pain has been one of the most troublesome questions, plaguing the best philosophers. People ask questions such as: How can an all-loving God allow the atrocities that we experience in our world on a daily basis? Why would an all-powerful God not stop evil if such a being existed? Or even the more personal: why is my life a mess? Oftentimes the questions arise from very personal experiences. The questions serve as a form of deep reflection, or venting anger, or blaming. Whatever the reason, people are asking difficult and pertinent questions, questions that the Bible was written to answer.

Accurately understood, the first two chapters of Genesis introduce the Pentateuch and provide a glimpse into life as God intended it to be. They answer the questions the Israelites were asking—the same questions we ask as we seek perspective for our own existence. There is an explanation for why our world is the way it is, and there is hope that it will not remain in its present state forever. God is working out a plan to reverse the painful effects sin introduced into our world.

Genesis 1 addresses the grandeur of creation as it reveals a God who speaks into existence a "very good" creation (cf. Genesis 1:31). God's creation was not simply "okay." God's estimation of the world he creates is that it is remarkable ("very good"). Even in its present fallen state the intricate details of the world are remarkable, and its beauty is unparalleled by anything that humanity has ever created or will ever create. As Christ taught the crowds, "Observe how the lilies of the field grow; they do not toil nor do they spin, yet I say to you that even Solomon in all his glory did not clothe himself like one of these" (Matthew 6:28-29). There is no comparison between the world God has created—a lily for example—and any of humanity's amazing creations—like a jet that flies. God's creation has been, is, and will continue to be the standard for beauty.

In this remarkable world, God planted a garden (Genesis 2:8-17), which was specifically designed and equipped for humanity. Although a rather clear description of this garden is provided, exact details of the life it offered are not clearly known. However, it can be safely assumed that it was a place of beauty and prosperity, where humanity experienced unadulterated blessings. Later in Genesis when Abram and Lot part ways, Lot assumes possession of the valley of the Jordan, which the text describes as "like the garden of the Lord" (Genesis 13:10). The comparison to the "garden of the Lord" is intended to emphasize the beauty of the land being described as well as the potentially abundant sustenance it would provide. The garden provides the ultimate comparison for any good place, the standard for evaluating paradise.

And the descriptors used for the garden indicate that it was a paradise. It was well-watered (Genesis 2:10-14), a necessity for continuous plant growth. The plants in the garden are described as "every tree that is pleasing to the sight and good for food" (Genesis 2:9). These trees inspired longing and invited people to eat of their fruit. They would create the response "That looks good!" So the general beauty of the "very good" created world was accented by a special garden created specifically for humanity to inhabit. This garden is beyond compare. To even begin to comprehend its glory, we must let our minds wander from the world we experience on a daily basis, to the kind of world for which we long. Apart from Adam and Eve, humanity has no idea of the paradisiacal nature of this garden. However, this is what God intended for humanity to experience.

Genesis 2 describes the particular details of humanity's creation, which Genesis 1 has already summarized and generically pronounced as being "very good." In this chapter God creates the man from the dust of the ground, fashions the woman from the rib of the man, and settles them in the garden of paradise, which he has created for them (Genesis 2:8, 22). In between the creation of man and the formation of woman, the chapter provides further details of the tasks God gives the man to perform because he is God's representative ruler in the garden. It also notes the concern of God that "it is not good for man to be alone" (2:18). The tasks are given prior to the creation of woman and are considered to be the responsibility of the man even though they are to be carried out together (cf. Genesis 1:28-30). However, because "it is not good for man to be alone," God creates a woman to be his helper (Genesis 2:18-22). Her responsibility is to be a helper to the man who performs his tasks as God's representative ruler in the garden. Adam's response to this new creature, which we assume was reciprocated is, "Yes! Someone for me!" We have every indication that the relationship was remarkable, even without fault. This is captured in the phrase, "naked and not ashamed." There was a beauty to the way in which the man and the woman related. Again, this is what God intended for humanity, but it is a reality beyond our present experience.

It might be helpful to expand on the beauty of this relationship between the man and the woman, but that would require the imagination. As those who live post-fall and outside of the garden, it is impossible to make conclusions about the perfect relationship they shared when the only reality we can comprehend is fallen, where selfishness prevails apart from the transforming work of Christ. Essentially, we can only accurately understand their experience to the degree we have known and experienced the fulfillment of our longings for life to be different. If we cannot imagine being in a relationship with someone like Jesus and reciprocating that kind of perfect love, we can never understand their experience. This reality is beyond a fallen person's imagination because a fallen person has only caught mere glimpses or small tastes of this kind of relationship, and only in the body of Christ. It is the kind of relationship that most people in this life are only able to long for. Legitimate longings actually provide an opening for understanding what life was like in the paradise of the Garden. Our longings reflect our design and purpose. God made us to know the kind of relationship that Adam and Eve experienced before the dreadful consequences of sin.

God creates a perfect world, especially the garden, and inhabits it with a perfect couple. "Paradise" is the only worthy descriptor of such a world, and any understanding a post-fall person would have of what "paradise" means would be insufficient. It seems to be a world where everything "worked" the way we would want it to. Deep inside us all is a legitimate desire for this world that "works." The reason we experience disappointment is that we were created for something far more than what we have experienced, are experiencing, or will experience in this present life. People were created for the paradise of Eden (or even better, the paradise of heaven), so any desires for life to be different are legitimate. More importantly, God longs to fulfill those desires. He is a God who wants his creation to fully experience the realities of paradise. This is the world God created (and the world he will again create).

The first two chapters of Genesis do not provide significant insight into the experiences of Adam and Eve in the garden, but it is apparent that "life as we know it" is a radical departure from theirs. Genesis 3 provides the transition from, or rather the "fall" from, this paradise. Humanity, in Adam and Eve, makes a wrong choice and becomes self-seeking, looking for fulfillment in life apart from God. God provided one clear prohibition for the man and the woman as they lived in the garden. Their violation of this prohibition brought about consequences that continue even now and will continue until all evil is cast into the lake of fire. This violation begins "life as we know it." Paradise, the experience that God intended for humanity, is lost...for the moment.

Before we investigate "life as we know it" further, let us look to the juxtaposition between the world as portrayed in Revelation 21-22 and Genesis 1-4. Revelation

21:4 states, "He shall wipe away every tear from their eyes, and death shall be no more, neither shall there be mourning nor crying nor pain anymore, for the former things have passed away." "Death" and "pain" are clearly connected to the fall from paradise as these two words summarize the primary consequences for the man and the woman. Revelation 22 mentions a river in the middle of the city (verse 2), "no longer any curse" (verse 3), and the "tree of life" (verse 2). Each of these reminds the reader of the garden as described in the first two chapters of the Bible. Note some of the following parallels:

GENESIS 1 – 3	REVELATION 21 - 22
heaven, 1:1	new heaven, 21:1
earth 1:1	new earth, 21:1
sea, 1:9-10	no longer sea, 21:2
Garden of Eden, 2:8	holy city, new Jerusalem, 21:2; 22:19
God's presence in the Garden, 3:8	God's presence among his people, 21:3
imposition of pain/difficulty, 3:16, 17-19	removal of tears, mourning, crying, and pain, 21:4
death initiated, 3:9	death removed, 21:4
the way/gate to Eden, 3:24	gates to the city, 21:13; 22:14
creation of sun/moon, 1:14-18	no need for sun/moon, 21:23

creation of day/night, 1:3-5	no need for night, always day, 21:25
"unclean" is driven out, 3:24	no unclean is allowed in, 21:27; 22:15
river, 2:10-14	river in the middle, 22:1-2
tree of life, 2:9; 3:22, 24	tree of life, 22:2, 14, 19
Imposing the curse, 3:14, 17	removal of the curse, 22:3
night, 1:3-5	no more night, 22:5

Revelation 21-22 demonstrates a reversal of the effects of the fall from paradise (Genesis 1-4) and a restoration of "paradise" to creation. The consequences of the fall and the evidence that paradise has been lost are removed as God restores his world. The reason is that God intends humanity to experience paradise. However, only those who recognize and confess their sinfulness and rebellion, which brought separation from God's blessings, and receive the free gift of God's grace, will be able to finally enjoy life as God intended humanity to experience it.

As in the beginning, the end of biblical revelation portrays a God who desires his creation to experience paradise, where relationship with him and with one another is fully enjoyed. Even though this is lost, God will make it a reality once again. This is a core concept in understanding the theology of the Old and New Testaments. The story of the Bible begins with paradise and ends with paradise. This demonstrates who God is and what he intends for his creation. He is a God who wants to bless his people with paradise.

God's major activity and involvement with humanity in the Old and New Testaments offers significant support for this theme. In the Old Testament, God is actively moving his people toward the Promised Land, a place of blessing or type of paradise. Immediately following the first eleven chapters of Genesis which provide the context for understanding the Old Testament, God begins this movement toward the land in establishing his covenant with Abraham (Genesis 12, 15, 17). This Promised Land is to be a place of rest, peace, and blessing. The report of the twelve spies gives evidence to this as they state, "it certainly does flow with milk and honey" (Numbers 13:27). The land was a marvelous place to live. An attentive reading of Leviticus 26 or Deuteronomy 28 clearly demonstrates that God intended for this land to be a quasi-return to the Garden of Eden because he wanted to immeasurably bless his people as they obeyed him. This is especially captured in three descriptions:

"so all the peoples of the earth shall see that you are called by the name of the Lord; and they shall be afraid of you" (Deuteronomy 28:10).

"and the Lord will make you abound in prosperity" (Deuteronomy 28:11).

"The Lord will open for you his good storehouse, the heavens, to give rain in your land in its season and to bless all the work of your hand; you shall lend to

many nations, but you shall not borrow" (Deuteronomy 28:12).

There is no doubt that God intended this land to be a return to a type of paradise. Even in a fallen world it is possible for God to pour out blessings on his people so they can experience the beauty of a blessed existence. Throughout the Old Testament, God's people constantly remove themselves from the privilege of being blessed, but God is constantly seeking to bring them back to a state where they can enjoy the privileges of his blessing.

In the New Testament, God is actively moving his people into the "body of Christ." The body of Christ is to be a context where they enjoy rest, peace, and blessing. Jesus' words in Matthew 11:28-30 bear this point out when he says, "All who are weary and heavy laden come unto me and I will give you rest." Numerous references in the New Testament point to the peace we are to have in our relationship with Christ. Ephesians 1 reveals that the

Father has "blessed us with every spiritual blessing." In the body of Christ, we, too, have the potential for a quasi-return to the Garden of Eden. However, this is limited by the abilities of the people of God to adequately live out their new life in Christ, for it is being a part of a godly body that makes this "paradise" experiential rather than theoretical. Even as godly individuals within a body that may not be evidencing godliness, we can know the "peace of God that passes all understanding" as we walk in the Spirit (Philippians 4:4-9).

In both Testaments the return is "quasi" because God has a bigger picture in mind. The bigger picture includes his eternal kingdom as depicted in Revelation 21-22. It is not until the end of the biblical story is revealed that it is possible to fully experience paradise. Neither the Promised Land nor the body of Christ is fully capable of restoring paradise completely. It will require the completed work of God and the eradication of sin for this to be realized, but God will make certain that day comes. Everything in life is moving toward this goal. Every event in the Old Testament is moving toward this goal. Creation waits. In fact, all creation groans (cf. Romans 8:22-23) "as we wait eagerly for adoption as sons, the redemption of our body." God will bring about a new age where he can bless his creation. He will restore paradise to his world for all his redeemed creation to enjoy. Genesis initiates this journey. The Old Testament carries it along. And the New Testament brings it to completion. It will happen. God will restore paradise. His kingdom will come. So, in the words of John, "Amen, come Lord Jesus" (Revelation 22:20).

Life as We Know It

The sad reality is that humanity does not live in Genesis 1-2 or Revelation 21-22. Tastes of paradise are only experienced intermittently along life's journeys and to varying degrees by each individual. Humanity lives in "life as we know it," which is the time period beginning in Genesis 3 and culminating in Revelation 20. This is the period that is introduced by the initiation of sin and terminated by the eradication of sin, as seen after the brief paradise of Genesis 1-2 and continues until the introduction of the paradise of Revelation 21-22. Sin impacts the paradise God creates and intends to maintain. As Genesis 1-4 aptly demonstrates, sin negatively affects both the perfect couple and their perfect world. Genesis 3 reveals the imposition of this reality as it recounts the story of the temptation by the serpent. The serpent creates the temptation that lures the heart of the man and the woman away from the goodness of God, who wants to pour out his blessings on his creation as they obediently follow him. After they are lured away and sin against God by eating of the fruit which they were commanded not to eat, they and their world are fundamentally changed. Consequences, both organic/natural consequences and non-organic/imposed consequences, are imposed and these form the core of "life as we know it."

ORGANIC/NATURAL CONSEQUENCES

First, the way they view themselves changes. They develop a new self-awareness. They now experience their world in light of themselves. They perceive that they are naked and that this nakedness is not good, so they sew fig leaves together (Genesis 3:7). This is the first instance of self-focused awareness and shame in the Bible. Before this moment, it is safe to conclude that they only experienced others-focused awareness, whereas now, self-centeredness becomes a part of their experience.

Second, the way they view God changes. They perceive that he is to be avoided and feared, so they hide (Genesis 3:8). Although we do not know much about their relationship prior to this, it seems likely their relationship with him was characterized by absolute trust and passionate communion. Their newly acquired self-focused awareness causes them to see God in light of themselves (anthropocentric or man-centered) rather than for who he is (theocentric or God-centered). God becomes someone to be feared and hidden from, not welcomed. Their new relationship with him is a radical departure from what they previously knew.

And finally, the way they view one another changes. They perceive the other to be a foe rather than a partner, so they seek to blame the other or something else (Genesis 3:12-13). This fundamental change is again enhanced by their newly acquired self-focused awareness, which causes them to see the other in light of themselves or as a competitor (egocentric or self-centered) rather than for who the other is or as a partner (others-centered). This is further developed in Genesis 4 in the conflict between Cain and Abel. Cain takes Abel's life because he does not appreciate Abel for who he is, but rather he sees him as a potential adversary. He envies him. This same message is reiterated throughout the Old Testament. These realities, which are first evident in Adam and Eve, continue in humanity via the sin nature. People are generally consumed with themselves and look out for their own personal interests rather than loving others deeply.

Each of these new changes occurs naturally within Genesis 3. Nothing, like a command from God, initiates them. They simply happen, with no explanation. They point to new realities, which now characterize humanity in its fallen state. The state of relationships on both a divine level and human level has been fundamentally changed. Inherent sadness enters the story and paradise is short-lived because with the birth of sin comes conflict.

IMPOSED CONSEQUENCES

In addition to these organic/natural consequences, the text also points to God-imposed consequences which are spoken to the man and woman in Genesis 3:16-24. There are both gender-specific consequences, meaning that God delivers specific consequences to the specific gender, and common ones, meaning there are also consequences common to humanity.

First, the gender-specific consequences[3] are clearly articulated by God as he approaches the man and the woman differently and delivers his judgments. He seeks them out as individuals, respective of their gender (i.e., created purpose). He treats the man and the woman in a distinct manner, and in the end they each receive separate punishments, although the specific judgment on each person also affects the other. The narrative sets forth the differences between the man and the woman and emphasizes the fact that the good and natural fit of these roles will now be convoluted. The result for each is the addition of difficulty.

The woman's appointed role was to be a suitable helper for the man and the mother of his children (cf. 2:18,

---

[3] For a fuller explanation of this section, see David Talley, "Gender and Sanctification: From Creation to Sanctification," Journal of Biblical Manhood and Womanhood 8/1 (Spring 2003): 6-16.

23-24). Her judgment then goes against the ease of being a suitable helper to her husband and the ease of bearing children. The punishment is in relation to the uniqueness of what it means to be a woman. It brings for her a life characterized by difficulty. Life is now not what it was intended to be.

The man's appointed role was to be the caretaker of, and the one who provided leadership in, the garden. He had a unique responsibility to God in that God specifically entrusted him with the single command given in the garden. The man's judgment goes against the ease of providing food from the ground. His judgment is also related to his created purpose and comes against the ease of leading. He is now forced out of the garden and into a world with thorns and thistles, a world that will require sweat. The punishment addresses the uniqueness of what it means to be man. It brings a life characterized by difficulty. Life is no longer what it was intended to be.

Note how the judgments are dissimilar, yet closely connected to the created purposes. For the man, who is "over" God's creation, the natural judgment is for his role of leadership to become difficult, which then requires he depend on God to fulfill his created purpose. So the ground brings forth thorns and thistles, which will require sweat to work, and the woman seeks control, which will require hard work to lead. For the woman who is "alongside of" the man as his completer and the bearer of his children, the natural judgment is for her role of responding to become difficult, which then requires she depend on God to fulfill her created purpose. The woman now contends for leadership with the man (who inevitably fails her), and she must now submit in response to him. Childbearing also becomes difficult and painful for her.

The first common consequence is that the man and woman are driven from the Garden (Genesis 3:22-24). They no longer have access to their paradise. Although the Bible does not clearly articulate the nature of this loss, it is obvious that it will result in something less than favorable for the man and the woman. The place that provided them with a special existence in God's created world is taken away. We can only imagine the losses inherent in this judgment.

A second common consequence is the inevitability of death, which will now be a reality for both man and woman (Genesis 3:19). They do not know when this death will occur, but it will come. They must live daily with the knowledge that life will end, but they will have no knowledge of when that might be. Paradise has been turned into difficulty.

ROLE OF DIFFICULTY

Life for the man and the woman is now characterized

by difficulty. This is "life as we know it." People do not live in the paradise depicted in Genesis 1-2, nor have they received the paradise that is promised in Revelation 21-22. Genesis 3 and Revelation 20 provide the bookends to our experience in this world. All of humanity, apart from Adam and Eve's initial days, has lived in this interim period characterized by the reality of difficulty, which is not given to simply cause problems for humanity. It is good in that the difficulty is designed to return us to God. God imposes difficulty onto the world to produce change in human hearts. Difficulty is a constant reminder that we are not in paradise, and it serves two purposes.

First, difficulty exposes our vulnerability ("my world is broken, and I cannot fix it"). When the man and the woman disobeyed, difficulty became primary to their existence, but it was not intended from the beginning of creation. This transition creates vulnerability for both the man and the woman. The essence of this vulnerability is gender-specific, because of the different created purposes for the man and woman, but both experience difficulty as they live.

In the paradise of the Garden they were not vulnerable, but in a world of difficulty their vulnerability was exposed. Humanity is deeply aware that all is not well and that we are powerless to change it. We have made many strides to make the world a better place, but with almost every change complications are introduced and unexpected ramifications result. For instance, I like my grass to be green and weed-free. I go to the store and I buy fertilizer and weed killer. I put it all over my grass, and my yard is gloriously green without any weeds. I feel somewhat proud of myself as I gaze out over my lawn for I have overcome this element of difficulty in my world. I am no longer vulnerable. I am in control. But the fertilizer is slowly working its way down deep into the soil until it finally reaches the water table at which point it contaminates my drinking water. Although my grass is green and weed-free, my drinking water is polluted and will make me sick if I drink it. Now I have a new problem to overcome. Despite my best efforts I still have difficulty to overcome. I am vulnerable. I cannot permanently fix my world. Difficulty is a reality for all who live in this world.

Secondly, difficulty heightens our thirst for this world to be different ("my world is broken, but I long for it to be fixed"). In the paradise of the Garden they experienced constant satisfaction, but in a difficult world their thirst was heightened because satisfaction is contaminated by difficulty. Humanity is deeply aware that all is not well and longs for life to be different. We have done much to make the world more like a paradise, but we never know what to do with the emptiness that follows our greatest accomplishments. For instance, a man can love his wife and enjoy their relationship. Some of his greatest experiences in life will be spent with this woman. When things are good between them, they are really good. But, for all the good times they have, they will have, to varying degrees, an equal share of disappointments. Disappointments are inescapable. A heightened sense of goodness in the relationship cannot be maintained. Both will be aware that, in spite of all the good, they long for more. They will be thirsty, and they will not be able to permanently quench their thirst in this world.

These two results, vulnerability and thirst, are intended to stir in us a desire to look outside of ourselves for more. They cause us to return to our Creator, the only One who is able to bring us security and fullness in this world. He is our life. Difficulty's purpose is to move us from trusting ourselves to the beginning of trusting God.

People no longer live in a paradise. Genesis begins the story. Genesis 3, the fall of humanity, reveals the mess that humanity has created by willfully violating God's command. Paradise gave way to life as we know it. After Genesis shows the devastating consequences of sin (Genesis 1-11), it begins to reveal the plan of God to deal with these consequences (Genesis 12ff). God will not keep humanity in life as we know it forever. He wants relationship with people so he establishes a covenant with a man named Abraham (Genesis 12, 15, 17). The remainder of the Old Testament will reveal how this develops and provide more detail of God's plan to restore paradise. Life as we know it will continue until God is finished restoring redeemed people to paradise, and he ushers in his plans for heaven (cf. 1 Corinthians 15). At that point, life as we know it will be done away with for the redeemed, but eternally intensified for the unredeemed. God will rescue those who have put their faith and trust in him from the mess of difficulty at the time he sees fit. Until that day, he is patient, not willing that any should perish (2 Peter 3:3-13).

Our Response to Life as We Know It

With this being our situation, how are we to respond to life as we know it, which is characterized by difficulty? Before we answer this question, it is important to remember the impact of difficulty on a person's life. Difficulty exposes our vulnerability, "my world is broken, and I cannot fix it," and it heightens our thirst, "I long for more than my world is giving me." The question, "How are we to respond to life as we know it?" will be answered in part by what we do with our vulnerability and our thirst.

If we are honest with ourselves, our strongest desire when we are in difficulty or pain is usually relief. Much of the time we simply want to find a way out. We just want it to go away. Recapturing the paradise of the Garden is no longer in our sights. If we can just find relief, we feel deeply satisfied. That is all it takes: a little satisfaction. If we thought seriously for a moment about what it takes to satisfy us, we would realize how little we are willing to settle for. All we have to do is take a quick look at our society, and we can see the baseness of our desires. "I can't wait until Friday night, I'm going to get so wasted." "If I just had a million dollars, I would be the happiest man in the world." "You're so lucky to drive that car; I'd give anything to have one." "Where'd you get that skirt? That is awesome." "I got tickets to the championship game; I bet that you wish you were me!" It does not take much to make us happy.

Now, back to the question, how are we to respond to life as we know it? What are we to do with the vulnerability and thirst that the difficulty of life as we know it brings? There are two options. The first is that we turn to God in the midst of the difficulty. This is what God intends. Difficulty is to drive us to dependence. The second option is that we turn to created things to deliver us from difficulty. In our foolishness we believe that other "gods" will save us from the pains of difficulty. Let us consider both options, beginning with the second.

It is our tendency as fallen humans to seek created

things or other "gods" for satisfaction and deliverance from pain. The story goes something like this. We encounter difficulty, which exposes our vulnerability and thirst. This is not a good place to be, so we naturally desire relief. In our vulnerability, we seek control. Getting control of the mess will bring relief. We cry, "I will fix my world; I will do whatever it takes to make my life work." As a result we pursue, crave, follow, cling to, and even die for, whatever or whoever provides us with a sense of control in the midst of our brokenness and seems to fix our broken world. These created things give the appearance that all is well, providing a sense that life is good or, at minimum, that life is getting better.

In our thirst, we seek satisfaction. We cry, "I want satisfaction, and I will find it now." So, we pursue whatever or whoever brings any measure of satisfaction. We drink from any well that offers relief as we live in the midst of pain. We settle for even the smallest quenching of our thirst. There are many quick fixes available, yet they all fall short of God's better plan. We typically pursue either sensual pleasure because the gratification is immediate, or personal fulfillment because these cause us to feel good about ourselves or our lives. And, once again, they provide a sense that life is good or, at minimum, that life is getting better.

Pursuing created things to find a sense of control and

satisfaction reveals the condition of our hearts. We are trusting in creation rather than the Creator (see Romans 1 for the exchange of this lie). What we trust is ultimately what we look to for life or what we worship. We believe that life is found in things or circumstances. "If I could just get that job, my life would be so much better." "If I could just afford that new car, then my life would turn around." "If he would just ask me out on a date, then I would be so satisfied." "If I could just get straight 'A's', then I will be somebody." "If I was just a starter on the team, then I would be so cool." "If I could just . . ." How we complete that sentence reveals what we worship. We all have idols, and we worship them. We look to created things for life, and we believe they are all it will take to bring relief from pain and satisfaction in the midst of life as we know it.

Isaiah 44:9-20 helps us understand our response to life as we know it and our desire for relief. It is a passage on idolatry with the goal of showing the foolishness of worshipping created things. In verses 9-13, Isaiah makes it clear that created things are made by created people. The craftsmen are human; they become faint and tired. They need food and water. In other words, an idol is made by a person who has been made. Verses 14-17a remind the reader of the fashioning of an idol. A tree is planted and grows; it is a created thing. When it is grown, half of it is made into firewood, which is used to keep people warm or to bake bread. Then, the other half is made into an idol to be worshipped? It is ludicrous to think that the same wood used for firewood is also worshipped. Why would anyone do this? Isaiah mocks this worship, saying,

> "He takes part of it and warms himself; he kindles a fire and bakes bread. Also he makes a god and worships it; he makes an idol and falls down before it. Half of it he burns in the fire. Over the half he eats meat; he roasts it and is satisfied. Also he warms himself and says, 'Aha, I am warm, I have seen the fire!' And the rest of it he makes into a god, his idol, and falls down to it and worships it. He prays to it and says, 'Deliver me, for you are my god.'"

The reason for worship is given in verse 17b, "Deliver me, for you are my god!" For you are my god. The point Isaiah is attempting to make is that looking to created things for deliverance is foolish. Yet we all do it, and we do it daily.

And what does it lead to? Joy? Happiness? Living the good life? No, the worship of created things leads to futility and emptiness. Jeremiah 2:5 demonstrates the outcome of worshipping idols: "Thus says the Lord: 'What wrong did your fathers find in me that they went far from me, and went after worthlessness, and became worthless?'" They ran to idols—"worthlessness"—and became "worthless" themselves. Verse 11 continues, "'But my people have changed their glory for that which does not profit.'" Their "glory" is the Lord their God, the one they are supposed to worship and look to for life. Instead, they pursue their empty and futile idols, created things that do not profit. Verses 12-13 summarize the first eleven verses, stating, "Be appalled, O heavens, at this; be shocked, be utterly desolate, declares the Lord, for my people have committed two evils: they have forsaken me, the fountain of living waters, and hewed out cisterns that can hold no water.'" To worship created things rather than the Creator is foolish. It is turning away from the fountain of living waters to drink from broken cisterns. Empty. Futile. Foolish.

This is not just the reality for Israel. We, too, walk away from our Savior, our fountain of living waters, to find satisfaction in our idols, broken cisterns which hold no water. "If I could just have _____, then my life would be good." To fill that blank with anything other than our Savior is to seek satisfaction from a broken cistern that holds no water. Yet, because of our foolishness, we return to the broken cistern over and over, lapping up whatever we can get from our created thing, but finding no lasting satisfaction. It is futile and empty, yet we pursue it fervently. This is what we call "addiction," and we are all addicted to our idols, though we are often unaware of it. This is why the Israelites did not hear the prophets' message. They were unaware of the idols that clutched their hearts since they were embedded in their culture, just like it is for us. We fail to see the grip material possessions, sensual pleasures, power, position, affirmation from parents or others, acceptance by our peers, vocation, awards, or accomplishments have on us. We fail to see how we worship created things, sucking all the life we can from them. Yet, in the end, it is a cycle that fails to bring us the control or satisfaction we desire. Our world continues to expose our vulnerability and thirst, so we pursue our idols with more intensity, more passion, and more conviction. We are addicted, yet we are empty. There is a better way that leads to life.

We can turn to the Lord in the midst of our difficulty. In other words, we allow difficulty to drive us to dependence and look to him for deliverance. Again, the story goes something like this. We encounter difficulty, which exposes our vulnerability and thirst. This is not a good place to be, and even though we naturally desire relief, instead we choose to walk by faith, believing that our Creator is sovereign over this world and benevolent in his dealings with us. We look to him and worship him, rather than look for relief.

In our vulnerability, we trust and obey. We cry, "My trust is in him. He will be my resting place as I walk through the brokenness of my world." He is Lord of all. Our lives are in his hands. He is a shelter for those who put their trust in him. Our world may be broken and we are not able to fix it, but we can trust him with all the brokenness, all the pain, and all the difficulty. He has revealed to us the path of life, and it is a narrow one. Yet, we choose to walk this narrow road in obedience to his revealed word. Life is found in him. We can wait on him to move in his time and in his ways and according to his purposes. He is great, and he is good. We must choose to trust and obey.

In our thirst, we wait expectantly. Rather than demand satisfaction now, we seek to live for his glory and according to his purposes. We cry, "I will wait for him to satisfy me in his way and in his time." As we long for more than this world can give, we choose to wait for him. He gives abundant life now, and we know the eternal life that awaits us. He alone is life and rest is only found in him. He gives a peace that passes understanding. We also know that he has gone to prepare a place for us and that this world is not our home. In the midst of the pain and difficulty, we wait for the day when he will restore all things to himself. Ultimately, we come to realize that satisfaction is not found in relief, but rather in him. He is life abundant, both now and forever.

This life trajectory reveals a heart that is looking to Jesus, the author and finisher of our faith, rather than looking to created things. We look to the Creator, the one who desires relationship with us. Who knows better the life we desire than the One who made us? The proper way to fill in the blank—"If I just had _____, then life would be amazing"—is Jesus. There is no other way. To look elsewhere will bring repeated disappointment. Placing Jesus in that blank makes him the object of your worship. He is the source of life and the only way to find joy in a broken world.

A couple verses help us understand that this is the correct way for us to live. 1 Peter is a book written to those who were going through extreme persecution. They experienced the pain of living in this world and being hated by it. 1 Peter 4:19 concludes, "Therefore let those who suffer according to God's will entrust their souls to a faithful Creator while doing good." In other words, trust and obey. Rather than taking control and looking to whatever brings a sense of control, we entrust ourselves to our faithful Creator. He can be trusted. Rather than seeking to preserve our own lives so we can experience control, he calls us to walk in obedience, laying down our lives for the sake of others. We are not, after all, the center of the universe. Instead, we entrust ourselves to the one who is and live obediently to his call.

Romans 8:18-23 reminds us that, even though this world is painful and we groan, we await a coming day when God will usher in his kingdom and restore all things to himself:

> For I consider that the sufferings of this present time are not worth comparing with the glory that is to be revealed to us. For the creation waits with eager longing for the revealing of the sons of God. For the creation was subjected to futility, not willingly, but because of him who subjected it, in hope that the creation itself will be set free from its bondage to corruption and obtain the freedom of the glory of the children of God. For we know that the whole creation has been groaning together in the pains of childbirth until now. And not only the creation, but we ourselves, who have the first fruits of the Spirit, groan inwardly as we wait eagerly for adoption as sons, the redemption of our bodies.

Notice the words, "eager longing," "in hope that the creation itself will be set free," and "wait eagerly." There is a day coming. We await that day, and we await it eagerly. Our experience in this world is not the end. It is not all there is to experience. If there is no more than this, it makes sense to demand satisfaction now. But, since there is a God who is seated on his throne ruling over this world, we can await the day when he makes all things right. And, oh, what a day it will be! We can worship him and give him the proper place in our lives.

What does living this way lead to? Does it also lead to futility and emptiness? Is it simply a bunch of "pie in the sky" empty promises? No. It leads to peace and rest. It leads to the incredible ability to be at ease in a world that is broken and guaranteed to disappoint. In Matthew 11:28-30, Jesus called out to the crowd, "Come to me, all who labor and are heavy laden, and I will give you rest. Take my yoke upon you, and learn from me, for I am gentle and lowly in heart, and you will find rest for your souls. For my yoke is easy, and my burden is light." Those who labor, toiling to maintain a sense of control or chasing after and demanding satisfaction now, are called to come to Jesus. They are simply to come to him, and they will find rest. It is only through Jesus that one can know a peace that is irrational (Philippians 4:7).

There are two options. Both involve worship, but the results of these two options are vastly different. One leads to futility and emptiness. The other leads to peace and rest. Not much of a choice, is it? Yet, this is a daily battle. Our natural inclination is to turn away from the Lord and to created things to satisfy us and bring us life. We tend toward foolishness, but we develop wisdom by daring to trust the Lord and his word. In a world of difficulty, rather than take matters into our own hands and get it all under control so we can seemingly have satisfaction now, we are called to look unto Jesus, entrust ourselves to him, obey his word, and wait patiently for his provision. By looking to him, we can rest in him. But the path to rest is the renunciation of our idols, idols that have worked their way deep into our souls. "If I only had _____, then life would be good." We repent of those commitments and instead commit to: "As long as I have Jesus, life is good." That is how you find rest for your soul in a broken, messed up, confused world, which is full of pain and difficulty. It is the only way, and Jesus calls to you, "Come to me!"

Making It Real

1)   Recall some of the difficulties in your life. How do they cause you to feel vulnerable (your world is broken and you cannot fix it) or thirsty (you long for more)?

2)   Do difficulties bring you to an end of yourself so you turn to God or do you simply find a way to work through it?

3)   What are your idols? Where do you look for life? Where do you seek relief? What created things have a grip on you and your heart? You may need to ask others to help you with this.

4)   Bring your difficulties to the Lord in prayer right now. Place your life in his hands. Look to him for life. Rest in his presence and grow in your ability to trust his goodness in difficult times.

5)   What would it look like to turn from your idols and turn to Jesus? What steps must you take for this to happen? Pray and ask God to help you.

CHAPTER SIX:
EXODUS

At the conclusion of our chapter on Genesis, we noted that the book ends with the account of Israel, in the family of Jacob, going down to Egypt (cf. Genesis 46-47; especially 46:8-27) and with Joseph's death (cf. 50:22-26). We also noted that the book of Exodus begins with these same two stories in summary form (Israel going down to Egypt, Exodus 1:1-5, and Joseph's death, Exodus 1:6). In addition, the first word of the book is "And," signifying a connection to the preceding book. This may seem like a little point to make, but it is important to note this little conjunction. This overlap creates a strong connection between the two books and demonstrates that Exodus is picking up THE STORY where Genesis ends. Noting these connections, we now begin our journey through Exodus.

The title of this book in the English Bible originates from the title used in the Greek translation which summarizes the main event in the book, the exodus or "coming out" of Israel from Egypt. The title in the Hebrew Bible is actually the first two words in the book, which is "and these are the names." As was stated previously, this title emphasizes the connection to the end of Genesis in the word "and," as well as to the origins of the nation in a family who came down to Egypt in the words "these are the names of."

Major Divisions

There are two major sections to this book. The first is chapters 1-24, which focus on Israel's redemption and the covenant. The second is chapters 25-40, which deals with the Tabernacle and the presence of the Lord. From a reader's perspective, chapters 1-24, are clearly the more exciting chapters of the book as they contain the major portions of THE STORY, which contains many powerful displays of God intervening for the nation of Israel. Chapters 25-40 focus on the building of the tabernacle with a few stories narrated along the way, which potentially makes it difficult reading unless you love architecture and building projects.

Exodus 1-24 can be divided further into two parts. The first part, chapters 1-18, concerns the actual exodus event. God redeems his people from slavery in Egypt. THE STORY moves forward like this: 1) the background and preparation of Moses (chapters 1-4); 2) Moses, Pharaoh, and the plagues (chapters 5-12); and 3) the exodus (chapters 12-18). Additionally, in these chapters we have two locations: Israel in Egypt (chapters 1-12) and Israel on their journey (chapters 12-18). The second part (chapters 19-24) concerns the establishment of the Mosaic covenant. The basics of this covenant are found in 19:4-6. In these chapters and throughout the remainder of the book, Israel is at Mt. Sinai.

Exodus 25-40 is a complete unit focused on the building of the tabernacle. However, there are a few events that advance the narrative (see, for example, chapter 33 and the golden calf). The building of the tabernacle is an incredible event for the nation. The whole building project culminates in 40:34-38, where God comes down to dwell amongst his people. This is taking the work of God redeeming his creation to an entirely new level. Although many readers of the Old Testament may not enjoy reading about the construction of a tabernacle, the significance of these chapters cannot be minimized or ignored. The end result, God coming down to dwell with his people, is fascinating when we consider the awful slide of humanity from Genesis 3 to this point in THE STORY.

Main Message

The book of Exodus begins with the people of God in desperate need. They are in Egypt, and their situation is not good.

Basically, the book of Genesis teaches how humanity got into a messy situation. With the introduction of sin comes a lot of pain in relationships and in life. From the first murder to the destruction of the world, people are clearly looking out for themselves at the expense of others because humanity actions were "only evil continually." In the book of Exodus, this situation continues as God's people are oppressed in Egypt. This is a dramatic turn from the fledgling nation's place at the close of Genesis—under God's blessing, with Joseph's status bringing privilege in Egypt. As a result, questions abound:

Does God care?

Why would he allow his people to be in this situation?

Is there any hope?

If God is all-powerful, why does he not act?

Is there hope of anything beyond the pain of sin and its ultimate consequences?

We ask similar questions when our world is caving in. Exodus offers answers as it demonstrates God's continued plan to redeem the messiness of life. However, before he unfolds his plan, he wants to reveal himself. He does this by allowing his people to experience an intensely difficult situation marked by pain and hardship. They are in slavery and will be increasingly mistreated by the rulers of Egypt. Through the hardening of Pharaoh's heart, God ordains the situation to get worse before it gets better. Pharaoh brings much pain to the nation, but God has them in this difficult place because he wants to teach them who he is. He wants them to know him cognitively and experientially.

God also allows this situation to intensify because he wants Egypt to know who he is and he has a plan to make this happen. He demonstrates his power over the gods of Egypt by bringing the ten plagues against them. God hardens Pharaoh's heart so that he relentlessly rebels rather than bow his knee. As Pharaoh rebels, the Lord brings more hardship through additional plagues. In return for the hardship Egypt had caused God's people, God brought Egypt increased difficulty. The Lord accomplishes two purposes through these plagues: judgment against Egypt and redemption for Israel. God makes it clear that he has not forgotten his people.

The ten plagues are quite impressive to read. As was mentioned above, these plagues demonstrate God's power over the gods of Egypt. Let me explain. The Egyptians, as well as other nations of the Ancient Near East, worshipped gods, who represented the different realms of nature. These powers were understood to rule the universe. For agricultural crops to grow with plenty, they believed that the god of agriculture, the god of rain, the god of the sun, and others needed to be satisfied or appeased so they would look with favor on humanity. They had to be satisfied or humanity would be destroyed. There are books where you can learn more about these gods and how God's power was specifically directed at them in these plagues. However, the main point to understand in the plagues is that God is displaying his power and majesty over the realms of nature to make it clear that he is all-powerful. The gods of the Egyptians are nothing before him. There is no god who can stand before him. He alone is to be worshipped.

Don't miss the implication of this: by displaying his glory in such a powerful way, he offered the Egyptians a chance to submit to his lordship. God revealed himself. He was no secret. Egypt could either respond to the all-powerful one or return to their wimpy gods in rebellion. This is one of the many clear expressions of God's mercy toward the Gentiles throughout the Old Testament. The display of God's power in judgment is always an opportunity for people to bow before him as sovereign over all. Egypt could have turned to him at any moment. In fact, Exodus 11:38 ("a mixed multitude") seems to imply that some did depart with Israel. They probably cried out with words similar to Ruth's many years later, "Your God shall be my God" (Ruth 1:16). The display of his glory demands the worship due his name.

God is obviously doing a significant work. He rescues his people from what is probably the most powerful nation of the day, and now he is going to enter into a deeper relationship with them. God had already appeared to Abraham and made promises. Now, he appears again, this time to the nation, to reveal himself more fully and to make additional promises. He initiates his second covenant, the Mosaic Covenant. As we will explain more fully in the following chapter on covenants, covenants have both obligation and promise. The obligation of this covenant is obedience to the revealed laws (Exodus 19:5a, 8; 24:3, 7). The promise of the covenant is relationship with God (Exodus 19:5b-6). Blessings and curses are a central part of this covenant (see Deuteronomy 28 or Leviticus 26 for a complete listing of these blessings and curses). God, in his mercy, shows his people how they can live under him and experience his blessings.

The initiation of this covenant does not nullify the Abrahamic Covenant nor does it contradict it. Rather, it more fully reveals who God is and defines what it means to love him and love others. Both of these loves were tainted by the fall, and now God is calling his creation back to the life he created them to live. This is the reason the Two Great Commandments, love God and love your neighbor, are referenced as a summation of the Law (Matthew 22:36-40), as well as the distinguishing mark of the church (John 13:34-35). The path to relationship with God is still through faith as revealed in the Abrahamic Covenant, but the Mosaic Covenant now defines what this life of faith looks like, and calls Israel to live it. As they live it, they will enjoy the blessings of God.

God is serious about this new relationship with the nation. He promises it in the Mosaic Covenant, but he offers far more than we can imagine. Rather than remain all-powerful but distant, God comes down to dwell with his people. But where is God, really? In the beginning we see God's presence in the Garden (Genesis 1-3). God is simply there (cf. Genesis 2:15-17, 19, 21-22; 3:8-10, 13, 14, 17, 21-24), and he is to be honored (in this case, "listened to"). There is no sense that he is absent. He is simply another character in the story. We also learn that his presence could be heard and that he is not just hanging out with Adam and Eve (Genesis 3:8-10). Adam and Eve even seek to hide from his presence (Genesis 3:8, 10b). The Lord "calls out" to Adam implying physical proximity (Genesis 3:9). After their sin, Adam and Eve are driven "out from the garden," but not necessarily from the Lord's presence (Genesis 3:23-24).

After the Garden, the proximity of God does not seem to change. He is still simply there (cf. Genesis 4:3-4, 6-7, 9-15). However, he is not just hanging out with them (i.e., Cain and Abel bring an offering to him, Genesis 4:3). They honor the Lord by bringing him these gifts and his response is important (Genesis 4:3-7; v. 4–"had regard for"; v. 7–"if you do well"). As a result of his sin, Cain goes "out from the presence of the Lord" (Genesis 4:16; cf. 4:14-"from thy face I shall be hidden"). This suggests more of a separation from his presence.

A major transition begins in Genesis 4:26: "then men began to call UPON the name of the Lord." After the garden but before Abraham (basically Genesis 5-11 and over 20 generations), the sense becomes more that God is ABOVE. He is still present in many respects (Genesis 6:3, 5-7, 13; 7:1; 8:15) and is to be honored above all (cf. Enoch, Noah, Genesis 9:20-21a; concept of righteous/wicked is defined by relationship to God). However, now "men call upon him" (Genesis 4:26), he "looks upon the earth" (Genesis 6:12, 5 ["on the earth"]), and he "comes down" (Genesis 11:5, 7). This is accentuated further when people are scattered (Genesis 11:8-9). During this time, people relate to God (Enoch, Genesis 5:24; Noah, Genesis 6:8-9, 22; 8:21), and God enters into covenant relationship with all humanity (Genesis 9:9-17).

From Abraham to Moses the Lord continues to speak

(Genesis 12:1), appear (Genesis 12:7), enter into covenants (Genesis 12, 15, 17), and is to be honored above all (Genesis 12:8). People continue to "call upon" him (Genesis 12:8), which points to the reality that God is now ABOVE.

The fact that God would "come down" should strike us a phenomenal. And that he is coming down to dwell in the midst of his people is a clear act of mercy (Exodus 25:8; 40:34-38). However, for this to happen, much preparation is required. Note the following:

Law—God makes it clear how people are to relate to him and to one another so he can dwell in their midst.

Tabernacle/Temple—God creates a "sacred space" where he can dwell separate from the people yet the people can have access to him.

Priests—ministers are set apart to bring offerings of atonement/gifts of gratitude from the people to God.

Cleansings/Sacrifices—cleansing must occur regularly to maintain the sanctity of the "sacred space."

Worship—God must be approached on his terms so he defines this for the people.

Purity of the People—sin must be atoned by blood sacrifice; the sanctity of the people must also be maintained.

This may not seem like the most exciting part of THE STORY, but we must stop to ponder the detailed preparations required of the people for them to receive the presence of this almighty and holy God. God's holiness is not to be taken lightly, by them or by us. After diligent preparation, the Lord comes down. That this happens in the midst of a story filled with so much rebellion is mind-boggling. I cannot emphasize enough the beauty of this moment. In other words, this is not boring or irrelevant information. It is absolutely essential for understanding the state of the world and the tender mercies of God as he continues his plan to redeem.

The building of the tabernacle and the detailed preparations necessary for God to come down and dwell in the midst of his people teach us a lot about who he is. We must see his holiness, his "other-than"ness[4] (Isaiah 6, 40-48). We must see his sovereignty over our lives. He is Creator, and all honor is due his name. We must own our sinfulness and acknowledge that it separates us from God.

---

[4] I take this term from R. C. Sproul's book Holiness of God. I think that it best captures the idea behind the word, "holy."

We cannot come into his presence in our sinfulness because sin turns him away. We must see the absolute importance of atonement in our relationship with him. Because of Jesus we have access to him and fellowship with him. We must be thankful for God's amazing work, especially in Christ. Yes, God is on the move again. He is doing the unthinkable as he continues his quest to redeem humanity for his glory. Wow!

Context in THE STORY

The book of Genesis ends with Israel in Egypt and this is where Exodus begins. Exodus ends with the nation at Mt. Sinai, initiating their new covenant relationship with God. At the beginning of Numbers, the nation is still at Mt. Sinai, preparing to depart for the land promised to Abraham more 400 years before. Numbers will focus on this journey, but the nation will not make it to the Promised Land because of their sin. THE STORY will continue with Joshua, where the nation conquers and divides their new land. However, Exodus moves the nation of Israel from Egypt to Mt. Sinai and supplies the details of the covenant and the building of the Tabernacle. It carries THE STORY forward, providing many details of God's power, goodness, and continued work with his people.

Looking Forward to Jesus

The unfolding plan of God continues in Exodus. The family of Abraham has grown into a nation. God redeems this nation out of Egypt and enters into a covenant relationship with them. This covenantal relationship includes many details that prepare the way for, and ultimately point to, Jesus. Mainly, it is defined by the Law, which is given to the people at Mt. Sinai. This Law is good, but it is ultimately paving the path to Christ (Galatians 3:17-26), who is the fulfillment of the Law. It is not sufficient in and of itself to bring people to the Lord.

The exodus is the major salvation event of the Old Testament, recounting the redemption of the Lord's people out of slavery in Egypt in order to make them his special possession and bring them into the Promised Land. This event was to be annually celebrated in the Passover, when the paschal lamb was offered in order to bring atonement to the nation. This yearly sacrifice comes to an end with the death of Christ, who is "the lamb of God who takes away the sins of the world" (John 1:29). As Jesus celebrates the Passover with the disciples in the Last Supper, he takes the bread and one of the cups of the Passover meal and tells them that he is the fulfillment of this event (Luke 22:14-20). The Passover was pointing to this future day when the Messiah would offer his life as a ransom for many.

CHAPTER SEVEN: THEOLOGY OF EXODUS

The book of Exodus emphasizes knowing the Lord. God brings his people through difficult circumstances so they can know who he is and lead them to place their faith and trust in him. This chapter seeks to bring the theological focus to the forefront to help you see how Exodus applies to your life.

In studying the Old Testament, it has become clear to me that God's primary concern is that he be known, and he wants his creation's primary concern to be knowing him. That means us! It is remarkable how often the phrase, "know that I am the Lord," appears throughout the pages of the Old Testament. He is God, and he wants to be known. Isaiah 42:8 states, "I am the Lord, that is my name! I will not give my glory to another nor my praise to graven images!" He wants to be known in all his splendor and majesty.

What does that mean? It means that we are to measure the experiences in our world, not by "things are going good" or "things are going bad," but rather by whether or not God is being known—that is the bigger picture. The issue is not whether your life is going well or not, but whether you know God or not. Ultimately, the things we want in this life may not become a reality because a greater goal is at work. This way of thinking gives us a perspective on life that allows us to live in the midst of difficulty. There is something bigger going on than our personal comfort and pleasure, and it is this bigger picture for which we need to live.

What is that greater goal? God wants to be known, AND he is at work in this world with the goal of making himself known. Sometimes we may like the work he is doing because it has positive results for us, but sometimes we may not like what he is doing because it appears to have negative consequences, which contribute to our own disappointments. BUT, we must see the bigger picture. Life is about what God is doing, not our own comfort, fulfillment, or even the granting of our prayer requests.

We want to learn from the broader story and glean from certain truths for our own lives. To accomplish this, we will look at the early chapters of Exodus from Israel's perspective and from the Lord's.

The Situation from Israel's Perspective

First, notice Israel's situation. Not only is it bad, it gets worse as the story progresses. In 1:8-14, the Israelites experience heavy labor in the midst of slavery. The blessings, which the nation experienced thanks to Joseph's influence over Pharaoh, are now a distant memory. They have moved from a position of privilege to one of oppression. It is important for us to feel what the Israelites are feeling: they are in a dismal place, and they are hurting.

The story continues in 1:15-22 with the king's pronouncement that all Israelite baby boys were to be slaughtered in order to curtail the nation's growth. Chapter one makes it clear that God is blessing Israel. Throughout the chapter, the emphasis is on "more" and "mighty." In other words, Egypt recognizes that God's favor is on this nation, and this results in fear. But the natural question that arises is: how could God allow this to happen to his chosen people? Why does he not act on their behalf? And, then, ever so subtly, God begins to move. The baby Moses is born and preserved. God is at work, but Israel does not initially experience it.

Have you ever spent some time thinking through this story? God's people are in trouble, and what is God's plan?

A baby! If a baby is to be the nation's deliverer, this means they are years away from relief. The baby must grow up to bring deliverance. This only becomes more complicated when the grown baby, Moses, slays an Egyptian and flees. When he is finally old enough to bring deliverance he commits this atrocity and runs off as a fugitive. As a result, God's deliverer is now hiding in Midian. It would be natural to ask: What is God up to? Is this the best he can do? God does not always work in ways that seem reasonable or rational. He has greater purposes than we can see immediately, and we may never see them this side of heaven.

Then, in 2:23-25, we read that God "knows" (2:25). This word, "know," is not referring to mere fact; rather, it is an intimate term, as in "Adam knew Eve, his wife, and she conceived..." God is intimately aware of Israel's situation, but he does not act immediately. This seems odd. But, once again, God has bigger purposes. He wants Egypt (cf. 7:5) and Israel (cf. 16:6) to "know". The play on words here is hardly accidental. God already "knows," but it is his primary concern that he be known! He is not in the dark. He is at work, but he works in different ways than we can see. So, God waits. He orchestrates events to bring about his intended purposes.

This waiting creates more difficulty for the nation of Israel. They are in pain. They want their situation changed. They are confused about why God does not act on their behalf. But there is a bigger picture, one they are not able to comprehend. We can see the bigger story because we can look back and read the whole story. We know the ending. But what about in our own lives? We do not have the complete story. We have no idea how things in our lives will turn out. For us, the bigger picture may not be clear. If we are honest, we identify with the Israelites' struggle.

It is into this situation that God calls Moses. He is the leader through whom God will deliver his people. There is some excitement. God is now at work in ways that can be seen. He has heard the cries of his people. In 4:29-31, the nation sees God's concern. They believe in him. They trust in him. But then their difficulty intensifies. In 5:1-20, the situation becomes even more difficult. Their labor increases. The nation must feel like God is toying with them, for what kind of God would treat his people this way? They want relief. They want a God who will fix their world—just as we do. This is normal for people in pain. But, when relief becomes our highest goal, we miss what God is doing in the bigger picture and that is why this story is important for us to understand.

For Israel, intensifying difficulty quickly turns their belief to contempt. Exodus 5:21-23 expresses Moses and the people's confusion. If God is so powerful, where is his power to affect change in their situation? Ever since they turned to him and put their trust in him, their situation has only deteriorated. In the midst of this despondency, Moses receives a promise of action from God; he will act on behalf of his people. So Moses tries to encourage the nation. But in 6:9, it is clear the people want nothing to do with these seemingly empty words. Today they might say, "Take your God-talk somewhere else." "God-talk." Their belief had become empty because God was not acting on their behalf as they expected him to. He was quiet in the midst of their difficulty, and he was not coming through in their time of need.

Then, as if the story was not dreadful enough, in 7:1-4 God tells Moses there will be more delay because he is going to harden Pharaoh's heart. What? Moses and Aaron demonstrate tremendous faith at this point by their complete obedience (7:6). But I imagine the response of the people was nothing short of: "What did you say? You've got to be kidding! Leave us alone!" The passage is silent on their response, leaving it to our imaginations, since it focuses on what is most important. God is at work...in his time...in his way...to accomplish his purposes. He will be known.

Let me make one more quick point before we move on. At this point, 7:7 states that Moses is 80 years old. 80! Do you understand what that means? It means Israel's difficulty has been going on for at least 80 years. It means God initiated this plan to deliver Israel 80 years before. It means God is moving very slowly to accomplish his purposes. He is in no hurry. His greater concern is the bigger picture. His purposes are above ours, beyond ours, bigger than ours. We must learn to submit what we see in life to something bigger. God is at work, and his ways are very different from ours.

The nation is in difficulty, and it seems like God does not care. But, in reality, God is doing something bigger than they can imagine. Have you ever been in this kind of difficulty? You found yourself waiting on God to do something, anything, but you did not experience any results? In fact, the situation was so dismal that you had no idea how you would survive. Have you been there? Have you ever had the feeling that God simply must not care or he would act on your behalf in the way you think he should? I have my students write prayer journals for my classes, which allow me to get to know their experience in life a little better. They simply open their hearts to the Lord and to me, so I can pray for them. I want you to have a glimpse into one of these journals (with the student's permission). He happened to be a Korean student who was wrestling with life's issues and his English is a little awkward. He writes:

Dear God,

I do this (prayer journal) because it is an assignment, not simply because I want to pray. God, I feel lonely sometimes, for I do not see you in my life. God, is it silly or ignorant to believe in Christianity? God, who are you? What role do you have in my life? God, my father does not talk with me as a father would. He might reply I am not as a son might be. God, how long will I have no green card? God, do you really "speak" through the Bible? God, I hate to hear these noises from the television downstairs or the television upstairs. The persons watching it might enjoy the sound, but I, in my room, dislike it. God, I dare to say that my life seems to lack significance. I am so insignificant. God, why don't you annihilate, or allow one to be annihilated, if one wishes to exist no more? Isn't annihilation as one wishes greater, better than he existing without end in conscious pains? God, how do you work in a person's life? In the world? What do you do anyway? Dear God, what is wrong with me? Why is there continuous contempt from father to mother? Why?! God, I know my father cares for me only to the extent of giving me large amounts of his sweat-earned money. Yes, it costs him hardship of labor and other pains to provide such money, but I wish he would have been less neglecting on raising me through himself, not just through his income. But it can't be any more. No, it can't be done. Dear God, I think there is no one whom I can trust. Maybe not even you, God. God, aren't you so cold and careless about an individual living on this earth that you cross your arms and watch him with scorn on your face?

I imagine that you know a little of this kind of struggle. To varying degrees you have walked in this man's shoes. Is God concerned with this person? Does God understand the questions he is asking? If so, then why does God not act? Is God concerned with Israel? If so, then why does he not act? He knows what they are experiencing, but he is silent.

God is concerned about Israel's condition, and he is concerned with this student. BUT God's primary concern always is that he be known, and he wants it to be our primary concern that we know him. It is not that God is silent or that he does not care. It is just that there is something bigger going on around Israel, and the student who wrote this journal, and around us. He is at work with the ultimate goal of being known by us.

When life is difficult for you, what do you want? Relief. Often we simply want to be done with it. The situation for Israel is deteriorating. They have had it with their difficulty and just want relief, which seems reasonable. We know what this is like, but our perspective needs to change.

The Situation from God's Perspective

In addition to the situation for Israel we have reviewed above, we must also observe the situation from God's perspective. The situation for Israel is not good, but we must become aware of the bigger picture. In 7:3-5, we see that God has a purpose for what he is doing. Actually, we will find this same perspective in other passages in the Old Testament. What is the situation from God's perspective? First, in 7:5, he is interested in the Egyptians "know(ing) that I am the Lord." This re-emphasizes his primary concern. To accomplish this, God hardens Pharaoh's heart so he can perform "signs and wonders in the land of Egypt." In other words, God creates a scenario where he can "show up" in all his glory. In other passages in Exodus, God acts similarly so he will be honored by Egypt (cf. 14:4, 17-18) and so they will realize there is "no one like the Lord our God." (cf. 8:10, 9:14). God wants to be known! He wants to be seen as he is—great and majestic. The bigger picture is that God is working so he might be known. Nothing will get in the way of this, nor will anything be more important. Nothing will stop him. He works so he will be known. The apparent problem, from a human perspective, is that this is accomplished through difficulty for the nation of Israel.

Second, God is interested in the Israelites "know(ing) that I am the Lord." God will eventually rescue Israel from their difficulty, but when he does they will have to fight against the wilderness, the lack of basic necessities like food and water, and other difficulties. God will continue to bring them into difficulty even after they leave Egypt. For what possible reason would he do that? He wants to be known! In 16:6-7, God provides manna so they will "know" that the Lord is the one who brought them out of Egypt. When Israel is in a vulnerable position in the wilderness, needing food to survive, God gives them a reminder of how great he is every day. He causes manna to appear on the ground with the dew. As Deuteronomy 4:34-35 states, "To you it was shown that you might know that the Lord, he is God; there is no other besides him" (4:35). God wants to be known!

Finally, God is also interested in the whole world "know(ing) that I am the Lord." It is not surprising that in the book of Ezekiel, where there are a series of judgments against Israel and the surrounding nations, the phrase, "know that I am the Lord," is used 49 times as the reason for the judgments. 49 times! God is not simply judging the nations, he is moving so they will know he has "shown up." He is unstoppable. He is unmovable. No one can overcome his movement. But, when God moves in this world, even in judgment, his primary concern is that he be known, and he wants the world's primary concern to be knowing him!

This is the situation from God's perspective. He wants to be known. What does that mean for our everyday lives? What does this look like in the way we live? In 1998, we moved to California from Illinois to begin our new position at Biola University's Talbot School of Theology. Because of the expense of moving, we left one of our cars behind for my brother who was returning from the mission field in Honduras. Upon arriving in California, we began to save for our second car. But, every time we saved a little, our older car needed repairs and it took all of our savings to fix it. One day, I accepted an invitation to speak at a church 40 miles north of Los Angeles. We left early on Sunday morning in order to arrive on time. When we were five miles from the church, our car broke down. We began to worry, but then God did the miraculous: a Christian lady stopped to pick us up and take us to church. When we arrived, a man who rarely attends was present that morning and he had driven to church in his tow truck so they towed our car to fix it. While I preached in the services, they fixed our car; and when church was over, we drove off in our fixed car, which cost me nothing because the church paid for it. It seemed miraculous to us. God was so good...but then, before we had driven one mile down the road, we realized the car was not fixed. And, upon further investigation in the days that followed, we found out that it was completely ruined and unfixable. As a result, we had no car! We moved from the difficulty of having only one car to the difficulty of having no car. What does it mean to know that "he is the Lord" in situations like that? What does it mean to know him? Can he be known even when life is not going the way I planned?

To answer these and similar questions, we need to consider the evidence. What is the evidence that God is being known in our lives? What in our lives proves that we know he is the Lord. First, humility, which is the opposite of pride. In Exodus 10:3, pride keeps Pharaoh from knowing that the God of Israel is the Lord. When we know that he is the Lord, we are reminded that what God is doing should be our primary concern. This results in viewing both the happiness and joys or the pains and difficulties of life in light of his greater purposes. This will cause us to step back and try to see what he is doing, to entrust ourselves to him and watch him work! We are to live for something greater than our present comfort. We are to live so that what God is doing is most important. He wants us to humble ourselves beneath the eternal plans he is working out in the world. He wants us to make knowing him and making him known our primary concerns. In

Philippians 3, Paul states that he can boast about many things, but they all pale in comparison to knowing the Lord (cf. Jeremiah 9:24). He states in essence, "I just want to know him, that's all!"

Second, obedience, which is the opposite of rebellion, gives evidence. In our Exodus passage, Pharaoh was living a life of rebellion, and throughout the Old Testament we see Israel's rebellion too. Rebellion is the refusal to acknowledge that God is who he is. But knowing that he is the Lord, or acknowledging that he is, will result in living obediently and recognizing that following him should be uncompromised, no matter what the cost. The call on our lives is expressed in Leviticus 11:44-45, "Be ye holy, for I am holy." Further in Matthew 6:25ff, we are instructed that life is to be lived for him, and in the process of living for him, he will take care of the details. Our primary concern is to know him and to make him known. It is about him!

Finally, worship, which is the opposite of selfish preoccupation, gives evidence. In our Exodus passage, Pharaoh was consumed with his own life and world and had no interest in God or what he was doing. The Israelites were only concerned about their suffering and misery. They were completely immersed in their present situation and could not see the bigger picture. They simply wanted relief and would bow before anyone or anything that could bring it to them. God wanted to direct their attention to him. When we know that he is the Lord, it should direct our passions toward the only one worthy of such love. It should result in the desire to worship, regardless of our circumstances because we are aware that God is sovereign and he is good. In Exodus 14:26-15:1ff, when the Israelites know the Lord and see his works, it leads them to break out in songs of praise. It is a beautiful passage, full of the testimonies of God's people as they respond in the only reasonable manner to the one in control of all things. They respond in simple praise, for he is worthy. God had not changed since the beginning of their ordeal and struggle. He was the same and would continue to be the same. Israel had changed. They knew life was about him and to be lived for him. If Israel had maintained this perspective, she would have experienced the blessings of being the people of God. But, when future struggles come, Israel forgets the greatness of her God and once more desires relief more than anything.

We are to live in worship. When our son, Andrew, was five years old, we bought him some new shoes, which had lights on the sides of the sole that flashed on and off whenever he walked. He wanted them so much. On the morning after we gave them to him, he got out of bed earlier than normal and quickly got dressed on his own without anyone having to tell him. When he came out of his room, I saw the reason. He had dressed himself early, so he could put on his new shoes. Without knowing I was watching, he began walking around the house staring at the lights flashing on and off as he walked. He loved them. In his own way, he was worshiping those shoes. He was completely enamored with the spectacular purchase. As I watched him walking around the house, so proud of his shoes, I smiled.

You and I both know how silly it is to worship a pair of shoes. But, you know what? We often become preoccupied by and live for insignificant things. Because we place importance on lesser things, we end up worshipping and living for those lesser things, rather than God. These become our focus. We become preoccupied with the wrong things just as Andrew was preoccupied with his shoes. Knowing that he is the Lord will result in worship. We are to be preoccupied with him, not the details of our lives. Life is about what he is doing—about knowing him and making him known. We must see the big picture. It's about him! Humility, obedience, and worship are evidence that we know him.

Consider the situation with my car again: what does it mean to know that he is the Lord? What would knowing that he is the Lord look like in this? It would mean being less committed to solving my car problems than in knowing God. It would mean stepping back from the situation and humbling myself before God, living obediently in the midst of difficulty, and worshipping him in spite of my circumstances. The only reason this is possible is that he wants everything in life to point me toward him. God's primary concern is that he be known and he wants knowing him to be our primary concern. The theology of Exodus shows how God is doing this. It helps us see the bigger picture of how God works and causes us to consider how he might be at work in our own lives.

Making It Real

1)   Think about the details of your life, especially the situations that are stretching you. Record your thoughts about these situations from your perspective. Now, rethink these situations from the Lord's perspective. What might he be trying to do in your life? What might he want you to know? Create a chart with parallel columns so you can see the contrast.

2)   For each situation, think more deeply about your response. It is important for you to understand and see clearly what your natural tendencies might be versus what your new life in Christ can manifest in you. For each situation, contrast and record what the following "looks like" for each:

- pride versus humility

- rebellion versus obedience
- self-preoccupation versus worship

Again, create a chart with parallel columns so you can see the contrast of each.

3) Ask God to help you be the kind of person who remains humble, obedient, and worshipful even in the difficulties of daily life.

CHAPTER EIGHT:
UNDERSTANDING THE COVENANTS

In Genesis, we learned of the Abrahamic Covenant, and in Exodus, the Mosaic Covenant. In order to understand the Old Testament and the relationship between the Old and New Testaments, we must grasp the purpose and progression of the covenants.

"Covenant" is a word we seldom use. If it is used at all, it is generally in the context of a wedding, were we will sometimes refer to a "wedding covenant." More colloquial words would be "contract" or "agreement," which are words most of us understand since we regularly enter into contracts and agreements. In a contract, we define what a relationship will be between two parties. Employers offer contracts to employees in which they articulate the responsibilities of the employer, like salary and benefits, and the responsibilities of the employee, like the duties to be performed or services to be provided. A car dealership offers contracts to customers that articulate what the dealership is selling, make and model, accessories, and price, and what the customer must do to assume ownership, the amounts of the down payment and monthly payments until the terms of the agreement are fulfilled. Both parties must fulfill their obligations or it will result in conflict and possibly end up in court.

The same is true with the covenants in the Old Testament. A covenant is simply a means of expressing, establishing, and defining a relationship between two parties. Generally speaking, there are two types of covenants, horizontal and vertical. Horizontal covenants are established between two people. This was common in the Old Testament world, so naturally we read of these throughout THE STORY. Vertical covenants are established between God and people. For our purposes, we will focus on the vertical.

In vertical covenants there are both promises and obligations. The promises come from the Lord, who initiates the covenants, and ensure the enduring nature of the covenant relationship no matter what may happen. The Lord is pursuing his creation with the goal of redeeming relationship with them. The obligations of the covenant focus on humanity's faithfulness to the Lord as the condition necessary to experience his blessings. The covenants also define the consequences of disobedience. Immediately, we are reminded from this that the Lord desires to bless his creation. He reaches out to them so that they can enjoy the promised benefits of relationship with him. Additionally, the Lord graciously communicates what he expects of his people so they can enjoy his promises. We must read the stories about the covenants with this in mind. God's intent is to bless, and he is doing all he can to help people enjoy these blessings.

There are four major covenants in the Old Testament: the Abrahamic, Mosaic, Davidic, and New.

The Abrahamic Covenant is found in Genesis 12:1-3, as well as Genesis 15 and 17. It is a covenant that slowly unfolds, with details being given along the way, and provides the context for the remainder of the Old Testament. It is a personal or family covenant because God enters into this covenant with a person, Abraham, and his family. It forms the historical foundation for God's redemptive plan. The promises of this covenant as outlined in Genesis 12:1-3 are land (Genesis 12:1; cf. 13:14-17; 15:18-21; 17:8), offspring (Genesis 12:2; cf. 13:16; 15:1-6; 17:5-8), and blessing (Genesis 12:2-3). The obligations of the covenant are faithfulness to God (Genesis 17:1) and circumcision (Genesis 17:9-14). These obligations point to internal and external realities. The internal reality is faithful living—the circumcision of the heart (cf. Deuteronomy 10:16). The external reality is circumcision—the circumcision of the flesh. With God the external is always an overflow of the heart.

The Mosaic Covenant is primarily found in Exodus 19-24, with additional details in Exodus 25 – Leviticus 26:46 and Deuteronomy 1 – 31. This covenant takes up a good portion of the Pentateuch because of its importance to the history of the nation. It is a national covenant because God enters into this covenant with the nation, including future generations. It is founded on the Abrahamic Covenant and calls for Abrahamic faith ("Abraham believed the Lord," Genesis 15:6). This type of faith is the basis for all relationship with God (Romans 4:1-5; Ephesians 2:8-10). Faith is always to be the root of our obedience; it is never a replacement for it or an option beside it. This covenant also provides a constitution for this nation under God. As such, it defined how they were to relate to one another and to God. It outlined their tax system and organized their government officials. The promise of this covenant is relationship with the Lord (Exodus 19:5b-6; Leviticus 26:40-45; Deuteronomy 30:1-10). The obligation of this covenant is obedience to the Mosaic Law as given to Moses on Mt. Sinai and throughout the early days of the nation's relationship with the Lord (Exodus 19:5a, 8; 24:3, 7; Leviticus 26:46; 27:34;

Deuteronomy 28:1, 15). The blessings and curses found primarily in Leviticus 26 and Deuteronomy 28 are an important part of this covenant.

Before moving on to the third covenant, let us pause to discuss the relationship between faith, as emphasized in the first covenant, and obedience, as emphasized in the second. Many people in the church characterize the old covenant as a covenant of works and the new covenant as a covenant of faith. Is this correct? Was Israel all about obedience while the church is all about faith? No. Let me explain. First, from our basic summary above, it is clear that the Mosaic Covenant assumes and is built upon the Abrahamic Covenant. It calls for Abrahamic faith. In other words, the obedience required in the Mosaic Covenant should flow from faith. Faith is the ONLY way for people to have relationship with God, and ultimately this faith is in and through the person of Christ. This is the argument that Paul makes in Romans 3-5, especially chapter 4. His point is that justification has never been by obedience to the law. It is by faith, and faith alone. Israel did not enter into relationship with God by keeping the law, nor do Christians today. They did not earn it, nor do Christians today. The Old Testament was not about works while the New Testament is about faith. Faith is imperative in both testaments for relationship with God. One comes into relationship with God through faith and faith alone, always and only. To believe anything less is to profane the gospel.

Second, God's goodness always precedes any call for obedience. For example, let us consider the very first law in the Bible. Genesis 2:15-16 states, "The Lord God took the man and put him in the Garden of Eden to work it and keep it. And the Lord God commanded the man, saying, 'You may surely eat of every tree of the garden, but of the tree of the knowledge of good and evil you shall not eat, for in the day that you eat of it you shall surely die.'" God provides a clear command with a clear consequence. However, in Genesis 1:1 – 2:14 God pours out goodness on humanity. He creates an incredible world in which he plants a bountiful garden for his creation. Then, and only then, does he issue a call for obedience. In other words, humanity's obedience should flow from gratitude for God's goodness. Obedience is worship, our proper response for all that God has done. It is the same in the Mosaic Covenant. God redeems Israel from the slavery under which they had suffered for generations (Exodus 1-14). He sets his affection on them over all the other nations of the world. He is bringing them to a land that was not theirs, and making it theirs. Nothing like this had ever happened. Then, and only then, does he issue a call for obedience. In Exodus 19:4-6, the Lord states, "You yourselves have seen what I did to the Egyptians, and how

I bore you on eagles' wings and brought you to myself. Now therefore, if you will indeed obey my voice and keep my covenant, you shall be my treasured possession among all peoples, for all the earth is mine; and you shall be to me a kingdom of priests and a holy nation." The Lord himself emphasizes that his call to obedience flows out of the goodness he has shown the nation. Again, the nation's obedience is to flow from gratitude. Their obedience will be worship, a response to all that God has done for them.

This same principle is found in the New Testament with the book of Ephesians serving as a good example. Hopefully, this will help you see a pattern in the way that God works. In the first three chapters of Ephesians, Paul outlines powerful truths concerning the grace we have in God through Jesus' finished work on the cross. Ephesians 1 is an incredible description of the wonder of the gospel applied to those who believe. In chapter 2, powerful truths, such as that we were dead and he made us alive, abound. In chapter 3, Paul expounds on the mystery of the gospel. These three chapters are a source of comfort to many Christians who need reminders of God's goodness. Then, and only then, does the letter issue a call for obedience. In chapters 4-6 we have God's call to obedience in the life of the believer. The believer is to:

4:1 walk in a manner worthy of the calling to which

you have been called

4:17 no longer walk as the Gentiles do, in the futility of their minds...

5:1 walk in love, as Christ loved us and gave himself up for us

5:8 walk as children of light...take no part in unfruitful works of darkness

5:15 look carefully then how you walk, not as unwise but as wise

A believer's obedience is to flow out of gratitude for God's goodness as demonstrated in the finished work of Christ on the cross and subsequent blessings. Our obedient walk will be worship, a response to all God has done for us. Blessed be his name.

Regardless of the testament, old or new, the work of reconciliation is the same. We come to God by faith. The only way we can have relationship with God is by faith in his provision. It is this provision which is growing in clarity throughout the Bible, not the means by which we come to him. We have nothing to offer him to gain relationship. Israel had nothing to offer him either. Obedience to the Mosaic Law did not bring about relationship with God. Only faith brings relationship. This is why everything in the Bible points to and anticipates Christ. God slowly unfolds his plan, but ultimately redemption is found in Christ alone. The Old Testament believers responded to the plan to the degree that it had unfolded, but ultimately their faith was in God's provision through Christ. As Romans 3:25 states, "in his divine forbearance he had passed over former sins."

Now, back to the covenants. The Davidic Covenant is primarily found in 2 Samuel 7, with references also in 1 Chronicles 17:1-27, Psalm 89, 132, and others. This is a dynastic covenant because it provides a perpetual ruling dynasty for the nation. It is founded on both the Abrahamic and Mosaic Covenants. The nation's king was to be an Abrahamic believer who lived under and ruled according to the stipulations of the Mosaic Covenant. Again, this is the convergence of the internal, Abrahamic belief, and the external, obedience to the law. The promise of this covenant is a forever throne (2 Samuel 7:12-16). The obligation is obedience to the already established Mosaic Covenant (1 Kings 2:1-4; 9:3-9; Psalm 89:30-37; 132:11-12). This covenant assumes the covenants that precede it as God deepens his relationship with his people. He is making his commitment clearer and extending them more grace as long as they walk in obedience.

While the New Covenant is normally considered a New Testament covenant, its connections to the Old Testament are foundational. This covenant is the ultimate focus of the previous covenants, for in it the redemptive program of the Lord climaxes. It is prophesied in Jeremiah 31:31-37 and 32:36-44, but it is not initiated and ratified until the death of Christ on the cross in Luke 22:19-20 (cf. 1 Corinthians 11:23-26). It is the final covenant because it is where God's redemptive work is directed and its final result is seen. The promise of this covenant is rest (Matthew 5:1-16; 11:28-30; Ephesians 2:8-9). The obligation is to be yoked with Christ (Matthew 5:17ff; 11:28-30; Ephesians 2:10).

Each of these covenants find fulfillment in Christ.

COVENANT	SPECIFICS	FULFILLMENT
Abrahamic	Promise: Land Seed Blessing Obligation: Faith in God's unseen promises	*prepares a heavenly home for us *the ultimate seed to "crush" the head of the serpent *lavished on us blessings in the heavenly places *clear demonstration of God's promises made known
Mosaic	Promise: Relationship with God	*his death provides relationship as he is the "way," we are no

	Obligation: Obedience to the stipulations of the Mosaic Law	longer enemies with God *fulfills the law for us
Davidic	Promise: Forever throne Obligation: Continued obedience to the Mosaic Law	*he has taken his rightful place on the throne in the heavens, awaiting the consummation of his kingdom *through Christ we are now new creatures who can walk in the power of the Holy Spirit in obedience
New	Promise: Rest Obligation: Be yoked with Christ	*Christ initiates and ratifies this covenant through his death, burial, and resurrection and calls us to new life in his glorious kingdom in which he grants us the power to live

God is working with a clear plan to redeem his creation. He is not moving from plan A to plan B to plan C. Each covenant fits together and moves toward the fulfillment of God's redemptive purposes. It is a beautiful plan. We are blessed to live in a time when we can look back and see God's marvelous work. Glory be to his name!

CHAPTER NINE:
LEVITICUS

While Leviticus does not advance THE STORY, which jumps from Exodus to Numbers, it is foundational for the nation and their relationship with the Lord. The building of the tabernacle and the coming of the glory of the Lord in a cloud were major events in Exodus and this tabernacle will play a major role in the life of the people. It is where God will dwell and where sin will be atoned. The glory of the Lord will also play a major role, as it is the cloud which guides the nation from Mt. Sinai to the Promised Land. Numbers describes the events leading to the Promised Land while Leviticus provides instructions for how to use the tabernacle. Now that the Lord is dwelling in their midst, what do they need to know in order for him to remain in their midst? Leviticus explains how to care for the sanctuary of the Lord and live in his presence.

The title in the English Bible originates from the Greek translation and means "relating to or belonging to the Levites." The book is given this name because it is a priestly operations manual, providing instructions for how to offer sacrifices and maintain purity in the tabernacle. It also adds important laws that teach the people how to live. In the Hebrew Bible, again the title of the book is its first word, which means, "and he called." This title points to the instructions the Lord provides the nation concerning the tabernacle or "tent of meeting" (Leviticus 1:1). In other words, the existence of the tabernacle leads to the instructions in this book. Now that there is a tabernacle, the Lord calls to Moses to give him the instructions the nation will need in order for God's presence to remain in their midst.

Major Divisions

There are two major divisions in Leviticus: chapters 1-10 explain how to run the tabernacle and chapters 11-27 provide additional laws for the people to follow if they want to enjoy the blessings of the Lord (cf. chapter 26). God is doing all he can to make his requirements clear to those who have entered into this covenant relationship with him.

We can also understand the book as referring to different aspects of the people's lives with chapters 1-10 pointing to the holy worship they are to offer and chapters 11-27 providing further instructions on the holy lives they are to live. These two emphases cannot be separated. Their worship and daily living were to have the same focus: holiness.

Chapter 10 emphasizes this point with the story of Nadab and Abihu, who offered "strange fire, which he had not commanded them." The Lord's response captures the essence of the book. He states that, whether in worship or in daily living, "Among those who are near me I will be sanctified, and before all the people I will be glorified" (10:3). God is holy, and his people are to be holy too.

Main Message

The book of Exodus ends with God "coming down" to dwell in the midst of his people in the tabernacle (Exodus 40: 34-38). In a simple reading of Exodus, it may seem that the phrase made popular by the movie, Field of Dreams, is appropriate for the building of the tabernacle. "If you build it, he will come." However, it is not that simple. Consider all of the necessary preparations that must be made. The law is necessary. God makes it clear how the people are to live so he can dwell in their midst. The tabernacle is necessary. God creates a sacred space where he can dwell and people can have access to him. It is a barrier of sorts to buffer the holiness of God from the sinfulness of people. The sacrifices and offerings are necessary. They enable people to remain set apart for the Lord, bringing reconciliation and allowing the people to appropriately worship and praise the Lord. The priests are necessary. It is important to have leaders who are set apart and prepared to handle the offerings and sacrifices the people bring to the Lord. The sacrifices must be handled properly as they come before the Holy One. Atonement must be made, so the handling of the blood must be explained. Since the offerings and sacrifices are coming into God's presence, clear procedures must be followed to safeguard his holiness. Cleansing is necessary. The tabernacle must be cleansed. Priests must be cleansed. The articles in the tabernacle must be cleansed. Sin must be "cleansed." With the presence of a holy God, proper cleansing must be a constant focus. The building of the tabernacle is only a small part of what must be in place. It simply creates the sacred space where God will dwell and supplies the environment where all the cleansings will take place. Leviticus provides the priests with the details necessary for maintaining God's presence. God in his goodness always provides instruction to his people. He does not leave us to figure it out on our own. Since this book is a priestly manual it can seem unimportant to the church today. We do not have a tabernacle, offerings and sacrifices, or the office of priest. We do not worship on the Sabbath. Instead, we worship on the day our Lord rose from the grave. We do not bring a bull to the altar of burnt offering when we worship. Instead, we celebrate the blood of Jesus Christ who offered atonement as our priest and then sat down at the right hand of God (Hebrews 10:10-18). We do not go to the Lord through a priest. Instead, the veil of the temple was torn from top to bottom, enabling us to come boldly before the throne of grace (Hebrews 10:19-22).

Though it may seem unimportant, it teaches about who God is, the care with which we are to approach him, and additional laws concerning living in relationship with the holy one. It also teaches about God's holiness, human sinfulness, substitutionary atonement, and cleansing that leads to fellowship with God. From these teachings, we come face to face with the glory and majesty of God. We learn more of his awesome presence. We see that he is truly other-than anything in this world. There is nothing common about him, and he is not to be treated as such. If nothing else, it serves as a constant reminder of what Christ has accomplished for us in his death, burial, and resurrection. There is no dividing wall between the Lord and those who belong to him. We have much to celebrate.

The main message of the book may best be captured in 11:44-45, which reads, "For I am the Lord your God.

Consecrate yourselves therefore, and be holy, for I am holy....For I am the Lord who brought you up from the land of Egypt to be your God. You shall therefore be holy, for I am holy." They are to be holy in their worship and daily living. Everything about their lives is to be set apart. Nothing is outside of this command. Their worship could not be divorced from daily life.

Context in THE STORY

Leviticus fits within the context of the book of Exodus, adding important information we would not otherwise have. In fact, it is probable that the events in Leviticus 9:22-24 immediately follow or are simultaneous with Exodus 40:29-38. Leviticus 1-9 provides a clear description of what happens when the tabernacle, which is now completed, is dedicated for use: Moses completes the work; the glory of the Lord fills the place (Exodus 40:29-38); the Lord calls out from the completed sanctuary with instructions concerning the use of the sanctuary; they offer dedicatory sacrifices and cleanse the structure and priests, following the clear instructions of Leviticus 1-7; and then fire comes out from the Lord and consumes the sacrifices (Leviticus 8-9). Exodus 25-40 focuses on completing the tabernacle which leads to the glory of the Lord coming down, while Leviticus 1-9 is focused on preparing the tabernacle for use by the people and showing God's approval by his consuming the sacrifices.

We find a similar event in the dedication of the temple in the days of Solomon, although the chronicler (the author of those books) has more detail. In 2 Chronicles 5-7, the temple is completed and a cloud fills the place (2 Chronicles 5:1-14). The chronicler adds that the priests were cleansed before the cloud comes (2 Chronicles 5:11). Then, Solomon offers a dedicatory prayer and fire comes down to consume the sacrifices (2 Chronicles 6:1-7:3). Following this, the temple is dedicated (2 Chronicles 7:4-7). Compare the two passages:

Exodus 40:33-35 and Leviticus 9:23-24	2 Chronicles 5:1; 6:13b-14 and 7:1-3
So Moses finished the work. Then the cloud covered the tent of meeting, and the glory of the Lord filled the tabernacle. And Moses was not able to enter the tent of meeting because the cloud settled on it, and the glory of the Lord filled the tabernacle. OFFERING SACRIFICES	Thus all the work that Solomon did for the house of the Lord was finished...the house of the Lord, was filled with a cloud, so that the priests could not stand to minister because of the cloud, for the glory of the Lord filled the house of God. OFFERING SACRIFICES

TABERNACLE	TEMPLE
And fire came out from before the Lord and consumed the burnt offering and pieces of fat on the altar, and when the people saw it, they shouted and fell on their faces.	. . . fire came down from heaven and consumed the burnt offering and the sacrifices, and the glory of the Lord filled the temple...When all the people saw the fire...and the glory of the Lord...they bowed down with their faces to the ground on the pavement and worshiped...

By comparing these two passages we can better understand what occurred. Regardless of the sequence, certain events accompany the dedication of any sacred sanctuary.

In conclusion, while the book of Leviticus does not advance THE STORY, it fits into the events found in Exodus. Leviticus provides a broader perspective of the tabernacle's completion and serves as the instruction manual for its use.

Looking Forward to Jesus

In God's unfolding plan, the book of Leviticus shows

us that sinful humanity can actually have relationship with him and enter his presence. This is only possible through the offering of blood, which brings atonement to the people. Sin is forgiven, but the people remain sinners. This offering of blood is sufficient in stirring the patience of the Lord until he can pour out the wrath that sin deserves on the Messiah (Romans 3; Isaiah 53). Sins are passed over until Jesus is crushed for the sins of the world. He stands in humanity's place and takes our punishment, satisfying the wrath of God, who must judge sin. Jesus is our substitute, the Lamb of God who takes away the sins of the world. Therefore, God remains just and becomes the justifier of all who put their trust in Jesus. The Levitical system was insufficient for permanently taking care of sin; it could only deal with it, and, therefore, the sacrifices had to be repeated over and over. Jesus, on the other hand, offered himself once, and then sat down at the right hand of God (cf. Hebrews 9-11). While the Levitical system could not take care of sin, it paved the way for the Messiah who could.

CHAPTER TEN:
NUMBERS

The book of Numbers continues our journey through THE STORY of the Old Testament. At the end of Exodus, the people are gathered at Mt. Sinai, receiving instructions from the Lord and building a tabernacle to house his presence. Numbers brings the people to the boundary of the Promised Land before THE STORY continues in Joshua.

The Hebrew title for the book means "in the desert." As a reminder, in the Pentateuch, the title of the books is simply the first word in the book. For Numbers, this word is not only the title, but it also provides a reminder of Israel's location, in the desert at Mt. Sinai, and a link to the previous book, where Israel was initiating their covenant relationship with the Lord. The English title, "Numbers," originates from the Greek translation and is derived from the book's focus on the numbering of the people, which occurs twice (Numbers 1 and 26), both in anticipation of taking the Promised Land.

Major Divisions

The structure of the book can be understood from a few different perspectives. First, it can be organized around the two censuses found in the book (Numbers 1 and 26). With this generational focus, chapters 1-25 focus on the first generation after the exodus, and chapters 26-35 focuses on the second generation after the 40-year wilderness wandering. Second, the structure could be organized around chronology. As a result, 1:1-10:11 would focus on the 2nd month, days 1-19, of the second year after the exodus (cf. Numbers 1:1, "first day," and 10:11, "twentieth day"). Finally, the structure could be organized around geography. The nation is at Mt. Sinai, 1:1-10:10, then the area around Kadesh, 10:11-20:13, and finally on their journey from Kadesh to Moab, 20:14-36:13.

For our purposes, we will organize the book around content. Chapters 1-9 describe Israel's organization. They are about to depart from Mt. Sinai after spending the previous year there. The census makes it clear that the nation is quite large (over 600,000 fighting men). To move a group this large through the wilderness will require organization, so these first nine chapters show how Israel prepared for their journey.

Chapters 10-36 chronicle the journey from Kadesh to Moab. The first generation rebels against the Lord by refusing to enter and conquer the Promised Land, and as a result of this disobedience, they are denied entrance. These chapters show the occurrences of Israel's rebellion, with the goal of demonstrating what the Lord desires from his people. The story makes it clear that the Lord is testing his people to see if they will obey him (cf. Deuteronomy 8:2).

Main Message

The main message of this book can seem a little elusive because there are so many different types of material. Like the book of Exodus, it contains parts that are very slow moving (for instance, chapters 1-10), but also some that are very action packed (manna/quail for food, the ground opening up and swallowing people, a talking donkey, etc.). But, overall, the book has a focus and seems to be written with the aim of answering a number of questions:

What happened to the first generation after the exodus?

Will God be faithful?

Will the people be faithful?

Will the people make it to the land?

How can the people live in relationship with the Lord?

The first 10 chapters of Numbers can be paired with the end of Exodus. All of this material occurs at Mt. Sinai and is focused on God entering into a covenant relationship with Israel. God calls his people into relationship, providing the core of the covenantal obligations and blessings, and the people respond affirmatively (Exodus 19-24). Then God calls his people to build a sanctuary so he can dwell in their midst (Exodus 25-40) and provides additional laws. With the covenant in place and the sanctuary completed, the people prepare for their journey, with God providing clear instructions on how they are to transport the tabernacle and how they are to be organized (Numbers 1-9).

Included in these chapters (Numbers 1-9) is a lot of what might be considered minutia, but it is an essential part of THE STORY, outlining for the Israelites how they are going to remain organized. The people now number over 600,000 fighting men, plus women and children. Can you imagine what it would be like to remain organized in a journey through the wilderness with that many people? These chapters include the taking of a census, instructions on arranging the 12 tribes in the camp whenever the cloud/fire would stop, setting the Levites apart with a clear outline of their duties along with those of the priests, a dedication ceremony for the tabernacle, and the celebration of the Passover at the appointed time. Other laws and instructions were sprinkled in as well, and all of this happens in nineteen days (compare the dates in Numbers 1:1 and Numbers 10:11-12).

Even though there are only 12 tribes who receive an inheritance in the land, there are 14 names provided in the census: Reuben, Simeon, Gad, Judah, Issachar, Zebulun, Joseph, Ephraim, Manasseh, Benjamin, Dan, Asher, Naphtali, and Levi. Why? First, Joseph was given a double inheritance, one for each of his sons, Ephraim and Manasseh. There is no tribe named Joseph; instead, two tribes bear his name through his sons, Ephraim and Manasseh. Second, Levi is not given an inheritance in the land because this tribe is set apart for service in the sanctuary. This is a result of the redemption of the first born at the time of the exodus (see Exodus 12:27; 13:1-16; Numbers 3:1-13, 40-51)

Then, God leads the people to the Promised Land (Numbers 10-36). This is the story of a journey, which is summarized in chapter 33. Reading of the various locations along the way is interesting and stirs to a desire to follow along on a map, but this just is not possible because many of the locations remain a mystery. In these action-packed chapters, THE STORY gets exciting and disturbing; and additional laws are given to the people as well. In these chapters we encounter the rebellion that prohibited the first generation from entering the Promised Land. In fact, rebellion is a major theme in Numbers. Numbers records two cases of rebellion against the authority of God's chosen leader: first by Miriam and Aaron (Numbers 12), and then by Korah (Numbers 16); and several cases of rebellion against the Lord as the nation journeyed through the wilderness. Despite the rebellion, the Lord is merciful, even in his judgment against his people.

Context in THE STORY

According to the dates provided in Exodus 40 and Numbers 1, this book picks up THE STORY immediately after the completion and dedication of the tabernacle. Israel is out of Egypt, and they have received the law, built and dedicated the tabernacle, trained the priests, and sanctified both the priests and tabernacle. The glory of the Lord in the form of a cloud has descended into the midst of the people to serve as a symbol of his abiding presence. It is this presence which will guide the people toward their destination in the years ahead. Through many tests of obedience this book moves the nation from Mt. Sinai to the plains of Moab, just outside of the Promised Land. The book begins with the first generation, post-exodus, and ends with the second generation including Moses, Caleb, and Joshua.

The book also ends with the nation of Israel on the plains of Moab, anticipating conquering the land of Canaan. Moses will die; he is not able to enter the land because he struck the rock rather than spoke to it in Numbers 20:8-13, and Deuteronomy records his last words to the nation. The mantle of leadership will be passed to Joshua, who has served by his side throughout the years in the desert. The book of Joshua will pick up THE STORY, focusing on the conquest of the land and receiving the inheritance.

Looking Forward to Jesus

The Old Testament message continues to point to Jesus in the book of Numbers. Most prominently, Numbers 24:15-19 references the rise of the Davidic monarchy, of which Christ is the ultimate fulfillment. As verse 17 states, "a star shall come out of Jacob, a scepter shall rise out of Israel," and further, verse 19 reads, "And one from Jacob shall exercise dominion." In an immediate sense (at least from an Old Testament perspective), this will be fulfilled through the Davidic dynasty, but, in an ultimate sense, this will be fulfilled in the last days when the Messiah ushers in his kingdom.

1 Corinthians 10:1-4 references the wilderness wanderings and "the spiritual Rock that followed them, and the Rock was Christ." Paul understood the very presence of Christ to be with the Israelites as they wandered through the wilderness, providing for them and guiding every step of their journey. The root belief of the phrase, "the spiritual Rock that followed them," was formulated by the Rabbis, who understood that the rock which appears at the beginning of their journey (Exodus 17:1-7) follows Israel before culminating in the rock that appears near the end (Numbers 20:2-3). Paul, then, understands this rock in a spiritual sense to be Christ. Moreover, Old Testament scholars commonly understand any presence of God in the Old Testament to be appearances of the pre-incarnate Christ.

CHAPTER ELEVEN:
THEOLOGY OF NUMBERS

There are many connections between the theologies of Genesis, Exodus, and Numbers. In Genesis we found that, as a result of sin, our lives are characterized by difficulty. God intends for this difficulty to drive us to dependence on him as we are forced to face our vulnerability and thirst. In Exodus we found that, even though we might find ourselves in the throes of difficulty, the "bigger picture" is that God wants us to know him. Our comfort is not his main concern, nor is it to be ours. Knowing him is ultimately what life is about. In Numbers, these truths deepen. We find that God is actively working to bring us to depend on him, trust him, and rest in him.

One of the central concerns of the book of Numbers is the wilderness wanderings, especially the repeated rebellion of the nation along the way. The main theological thrust of the book is that God's miraculous works were signs intended to produce belief. In Numbers 14:11, the Lord says to Moses, "How long will this people despise me? And how long will they not believe in me, in spite of all the signs that I have done among them?" The Lord makes it clear that his miraculous works are to result in belief. He wants Israel to know who he is and for the way they live to demonstrate their knowledge. Over and over, God allows Israel to experience difficulty, then miraculously delivers them with signs intended to stir their trust in him.

We see this focus throughout THE STORY. When the Lord calls Moses to go to the people and lead them out of Egypt to the Promised Land, he provides three signs intended to confirm his calling and produce belief: 1) his staff became a serpent, but, when he picked it up by the tail it became a staff again; 2) when he put his hand inside his cloak, it became leprous, but, when he reinserted his hand it was restored; and 3) he poured water from the Nile on the ground and it became blood. In this case, the intended result, belief, comes about. Exodus 4:30-31 states, "Aaron spoke all the words that the Lord had spoken to Moses and did the signs in the sight of the people. And the people believed; and when they heard that the Lord had visited the people of Israel and that he had seen their affliction, they bowed their heads and worshiped." Israel sees the sign and it produced belief. We see a similar positive response with the sign of the parting of the Red Sea. The Lord leads the people out of Egypt, but then hardens Pharaoh's heart so that he pursues them. When they are trapped with the Egyptian army in close pursuit, Moses says, "Fear not, stand firm, and see the salvation of the Lord, which he will work for you today. For the Egyptians whom you see today, you shall never see again. The Lord will fight for you, and you have only to be silent" (Exodus 14:13-14). Moses performs the sign by stretching out his hand over the sea. The Egyptian army is destroyed, and Israel is miraculously preserved. Exodus 14:30-31 summarizes the story: "Thus the Lord saved Israel that day from the hand of the Egyptians, and Israel saw the Egyptians dead on the seashore. Israel saw the great power that the Lord used against the Egyptians, so the people feared the Lord, and they believed in the Lord and in his servant Moses." In other words, Israel saw the sign, and it produced belief.

We learned from Genesis that this world is rigged with difficulty to turn people to the Lord. We learned from Exodus that when God's people are in difficult situations, God desires them to know that he is the Lord. He is great and mighty. Knowing was to result in trust and an awareness of the bigger picture God is working out. And now, we learn in Numbers that God puts his people in difficult situations so that they can witness his miraculous provision and grow in belief. Exodus 16:4 shows that the manna was given only as a daily provision so "that I may test them, whether they will walk in my law or not." God brought tests to help his people grow in dependence upon him.

Let us explore this theological point further beginning with Numbers 14:11: "And the Lord said to Moses, 'How long will this people despise me? And how long will they not believe in me, in spite of all the signs that I have done among them?'" The Lord is disappointed because he has offered signs, but the people lack belief. After the Lord responds to Moses' pleas and pardons the people for their rebellion, he says in Numbers 14:21,

But truly, as I live, and as all the earth shall be filled with the glory of the Lord, none of the men who have seen my glory and my signs that I did in Egypt and in the wilderness, and yet have put me to the test these ten times and have not obeyed my voice, shall see the land that I swore to give to their fathers. And none of those who despised me shall see it. But my servant Caleb, because he has a different spirit and has followed me fully, I will bring into the land into which he went, and his descendants shall possess it.

The people have not obeyed the Lord because the signs have not led to belief. The Lord reacts strongly against the people saying, "And none of those who despised me shall see it." God intends signs to produce belief.

What are the "ten times" in 14:21? Rabbis have deliberated over this issue for years with some concluding that this is hyperbole used to make a point, similar to a father who says to his children, "I've told you a hundred times to clean your room!" This isn't an exact count, but is intended to emphasize that the children have been reminded many times. Similarly, God is not counting the exact number of tests, he is simply making it clear that he has been patient with them. However, some Rabbis have concluded that this is an exact count. Let us pause for moment and search the text to see if we can find the ten times in the story? Remember that the book of Leviticus is not included in this study, so you may skip that book in your search. Before you proceed, take a few minutes to see what you can find.

Using Exodus 14 – Numbers 14 as our boundaries, note that there are a possible ten times in THE STORY. Obviously, there is debate, but consider the following:

PASSAGE	SUMMARY
Exodus 14:10-12	At the Red Sea where they feared

that Pharaoh's army would destroy them

Exodus 15:22-24　At Marah where they found bitter water and grumbled

Exodus 16:1-3　In the Desert of Sin as they hungered and grumbled

Exodus 16:19-20　In the Desert of Sin as they paid no attention to Moses concerning the storing of the manna until the morning—they kept some as assurance

Exodus 16:27-30　In the Desert of Sin as they disregarded Moses concerning the gathering of the manna on the seventh day—they did attempt to gather for assurance

Exodus 17:1-4　At Rephidim as they quarreled and grumbled about water

Exodus 32:1-35　At Mount Sinai as Aaron led the people in making the golden calf as their "god"

Numbers 11:1-3　At Taberah where the people complained to the Lord

Numbers 11:4-34　At Kibroth Hattaavah in the complaining provoked by the rabble about manna

Numbers 14:1-3   At Kadesh in the Desert of Paran
when the people refused to receive
the good report of Joshua and
Caleb but rather complained about
their plight

God produced signs previous to each difficult incident that were sufficient to generate belief despite the difficulties they were facing. Imagine having witnessed the power of God in the 10 plagues, yet not believing that God could spare them from the Egyptian army pursuing them. But God in his mercy provides them with another sign by parting the Red Sea. Imagine having walked through the middle of the Red Sea on dry ground, yet not believing that God could provide clean water instead of bitter. In fact, how long do you think it would take you to lose confidence in God after witnessing all this? Seriously, how many? A year? Six months? One month? A week? How long did it take Israel? Exodus 15:22 says they were a mere three days into their wilderness journey. Three days until they began complaining instead of believing based on the signs they had seen. But God in his mercy provides them with another sign by purifying the water. Imagine having seen the water purified, yet not believing that God could provide food for the journey. But God in his mercy provides manna for them, with the promise of daily provision until they eat the fruit of the land. Wow! God is bending over backwards to demonstrate his goodness to his people. He is being patient, gently helping them in their lack of belief. However, God is not in the business of proving himself each time his people encounter something painful. He wants us to rely on the history of his faithfulness as found in the Bible and in our own lives. He has provided us with sufficient signs that our lives should evidence belief.

The issue throughout the stories is captured in Numbers 11:23: "Is the Lord's hand shortened? Now you shall see whether my word will come true or not." The question is whether or not the Lord's power is enough. Regardless of the difficulty, the Lord wanted them to see him as sufficient in the midst of their difficulty. Deuteronomy 5:29 gives the central concern of the Lord: "Oh that they had such a mind as this always, to fear me and to keep all my commandments, that it might go well with them and with their descendants forever!" This is the belief the Lord desired. His signs were intended to gain their trust.

The New Testament picks up on this same theme. Mark 6:33-52 is one such instance. By this point in the book, Jesus had called his disciples and they had witnessed his power and authority over this world in the form of miracles on numerous occasions. These miracles were the signs. In Mark 6, Jesus gives them a test similar to what we have seen in the Old Testament. His glory and his signs are to produce a belief that affects the way the disciples live. They are to know that he is the Lord and to live in a way that demonstrates complete trust and obedience. In Mark 6:35-36, the disciples encourage Jesus to send the crowds away so that they can go to the surrounding villages and buy food. Remember that there were 5,000 men in the crowd (Mark 6:44). Then in Mark 6:37, Jesus tests his disciples, commanding them to give the people something to eat. Rather than bowing at his feet in trust and submitting to Jesus' plans, which would acknowledge that they knew he was the Lord, their response focuses only on how much it would cost to purchase that much bread. They fail the test. At Jesus' request they go and see how much food they can find amongst the crowd, and they return with five biscuits and two fish (Mark 6:38). Jesus then blesses the food, breaks it, and gives it to the people. When the meal is over, there are twelve full baskets of broken pieces of bread and fish. The disciples had now witnessed a mighty act and the knowledge of this mighty act was to affect the way they lived. It was intended to generate complete trust in the one they followed. They were to be forever transformed by such a revelation of the person of the Lord.

The passage continues with Jesus walking on water

(Mark 6:45-52). The scene begins with Jesus separating from the disciples for a time of prayer. He commands the disciples to go to the other side of the lake, and as they are going, they encounter a difficult storm (Mark 6:48). Jesus offers them another test. He walks out on the water and, as the passage states, "he intended to pass them by." The disciples see him and, rather than acknowledge that he is the Lord and has all power over all creation, they are "frightened" (Mark 6:50). He comes to the boat, and as he gets in with them and the winds suddenly cease, they are "greatly astonished" (Mark 6:51). Then Mark writes, "for they had not gained any insight from the incident of the loaves, but their heart was hardened" (Mark 6:52). Not knowing who the Lord is, as shown by a lack of trust and disobedience, is equated with hardness of heart. Had they "gained insight" they would have known who Jesus is and how he could walk on water. Their response should have been, "Hey, Jesus, is this storm going to continue on or are you going to stop it and give us a break?" or "Hey, Jesus, do you mind if we abandon the boat and just walk with you?" or more realistically for fallen humanity, "Hey, Jesus, help us in our unbelief." To know that Jesus is Lord would have dramatically affected their lives and should have such an effect on our lives as well.

Later, the disciples and Jesus again encounter a large crowd of people at mealtime. Note what Jesus says, "I feel compassion for the multitude because they have remained with me now three days, and have nothing to eat; and if I send them away hungry to their home, they will faint on the way; and some of them have come from a distance" (Mark 8:2). This is another test. If the disciples had known that he is the Lord, they would simply bow at Jesus' feet and submit to his instructions. Again, they fail the test and say, "Where will anyone be able to find enough to satisfy these men with bread here in a desolate place?" (Mark 8:4). Once again Jesus asks them how much bread they have, and the disciples answer, seven biscuits (Mark 8:5) and a few small fish (Mark 8:7). 4,000 men were served (Mark 8:9) and they gathered seven large baskets as leftovers (Mark 8:8).

Soon after this, the disciples begin to discuss the fact that they have no bread (Mark 8:16). They are with a man who has fed 5,000 men with five biscuits and two fish with baskets full left over, walked on water and calmed a storm, and fed 4,000 men with seven biscuits and a few small fish, again with baskets full left over. To know that he is the Lord would mean going to him in their need and trusting his provision. Jesus promptly interrupts their conversation with some pointed questions,

"Why do you discuss the fact that you have no bread? Do you not yet see or understand?

Do you have a hardened heart?

Having eyes do you not see?

Having ears do you not hear?

Do you not remember, when I broke the five loaves for the five thousand, how many baskets full of broken pieces you picked up?

And when I broke the seven for the four thousand, how many baskets full of broken pieces you picked up?

Do you not yet understand?"

Jesus is making it plain that knowing who he is will affect the way we look at and respond to life. To know that Jesus is Lord will result in a life of complete trust and obedience. That is what he wanted from his disciples. His question to them, "Do you not yet understand?" should ring in our ears today. Do we?

Hopefully, this makes it obvious that the Lord is seeking to transform us into a people who bow the knee to him and trust him completely. We are not to live in fear. We are not to cower before the difficulties of life. We are not to shrink back from adversity. We can live with boldness because we know that he is the Lord. He has given us the signs we need, both in the Bible and in our own lives, to live with profound belief. That is the theology of Numbers. Is it not amazing how relevant these

Old Testament books are to our lives? Blessed be the name of the Lord for providing us with such food on which to feast.

Making It Real

1)   Consider the difficulties you have faced. How have you responded? Do you put the Lord to the test by your response? Write about an event in which you did not have a good response.

2)   Look at the proposed list of ten times. What would belief look like? If God's previous signs had the intended effect, what would Israel's responses have been? Remember, difficulty exposes our vulnerability and thirst.

3)   Exodus 14:10-14 and Deuteronomy 1:26-33 will help you see faith by looking at Moses' response. Pray for this kind of faith in your own life. Now consider the teaching of Numbers, signs are to produce belief. What do you think your response would be if you "believed" that he is the Lord and that he is faithful? Pray that God would help you with this.

4)   For your own encouragement, write down the many ways God was faithful to his people throughout the Bible. Add clear examples of faithfulness from your own life. Meditate on these. Praise him for his goodness. Let them build your faith for difficult times.

CHAPTER TWELVE:
DEUTERONOMY

The book of Deuteronomy is not part of THE STORY, but is concurrent with the events of Numbers. The name of the book in the Hebrew is, once again, the first word in the book, which means "and these are the words" or literally, "the words." More specifically, the book begins with the words which "Moses spoke to all Israel beyond the Jordan in the wilderness..." (Deuteronomy 1:1). The contents concern specific words spoken in a specific location, at a specific time. The title in our English Bibles originates from the Greek translation and means "second law," which is a reference to the second giving of the Law in chapter five as well as the many other laws included throughout the book.

Major Divisions

The book of Deuteronomy has a very basic message and the structure underscores this. There are three sermons, or groupings of material, which begin in 1:1, 5:1, and 29:1. We can entitle the sermons: "Historical Reflections," 1:1 – 4:49; "The Call to Be God's People," 5:1 – 28:68; and "Covenant Renewal and Blessing," 29:1 – 34:12.

We can break the longest sermon, "The Call to Be God's People" (5:1 – 28:68), into two parts. The first part, "The Commandments" in chapters 5-26, is the longest because there are many that must still be communicated to the nation. The first generation died in the wilderness, so communicating the covenant and all its stipulations to the second generation before they enter the Promised Land is essential. The second part, "Blessings and Curses" in chapters 27-28, communicates the blessings God will heap on his people if they follow him in obedience; however, he also makes it clear that there are painful consequences for rebellion. God, in his mercy, is initially gentle in his punishment. But, because God is a God of love, the punishment increases as necessary to get Israel's attention and turn them back to him.

Main Message

The main message of this book is focused on restating the Law, as given by Moses, and reaffirming the covenant, since this is the second generation. It serves as the end of this unit we call the Pentateuch. This is Moses' final address to the nation, which will enter the Promised Land without him. Remember, Moses is not allowed to enter because he profaned the Lord by striking the rock rather than speaking to it (Numbers 20:8-13). Moses is now an old man. He has walked with this nation as their leader for the duration of the 40-year wilderness wandering. He has been a shepherd to them. He has sought to help them live in obedience to the covenant. He has been faithful to God and to the people. The journey from Mt. Horeb (another name for Mt. Sinai which is used throughout Deuteronomy) to the Promised Land was a mere "eleven days' journey" (Deuteronomy 1:2), but because of the rebellion of the nation (Numbers 14) they wandered for 40 years. Moses was with them the whole way, and now he passes on his final bit of wisdom.

Now that we have reached the book of Deuteronomy, we see that the Pentateuch spans from creation up to the nation's preparations for entering the Promised Land. However, all of it was written for the first and second generation as a unit. It is both an introduction showing their origins (Genesis 1 – Exodus 3) and a history of their lives (Exodus 4 – Deuteronomy 34).

As noted above, the first sermon of Deuteronomy (1:1 – 4:49, "Historical Reflections") is a reflection on the nation's history with a focus on the time after the exodus, specifically when they left Mt. Sinai (beginning in Numbers 10). Historical reflection is not simply retelling the events; it is always theological at its core. Thus, this reflection is intended to stir in Israel a desire to trust the Lord so they can conquer the land as he commanded. Moses refers to specific instances of God's faithfulness to inspire the people to trust:

4:3   "Your eyes have seen what the Lord did at Baal-peor, for the Lord your God destroyed from among you all the men who followed the Baal of Peor."

4:10   "...how on the day that you stood before the Lord your God at Horeb, the Lord said to me, 'Gather the people to me, that I may let them hear my words, so that they may learn to fear me....'"

4:11-15   "you came near and stood at the foot of the mountain...the Lord spoke to you....you heard the sound of words...he declared to you his covenant...he wrote them on two tablets of stone...."

4:20   "the Lord has taken you and brought you out of the iron furnace, out of Egypt, to be a people of his own inheritance..."

4:21   "the Lord was angry with me because of you..."

4:32-40 "For ask now of the days that are past, which were before you, since the day that God created man on the earth...hear the voice of a god speaking out of the midst of the first...has any god ever attempted to go and take a nation for himself from the midst of another nation, by trials, by signs, by wonders, and by war, by a mighty hand and an outstretched arm, and by great deeds of terror, all of which the Lord your God did for you in Egypt before your eyes?...driving out before you nations greater and mightier than yourselves...."

Exhortations flow from these events with the intention of urging the people to faithful obedience:

4:9   "only take care, and keep your soul diligently, lest you forget the things your eyes have seen"

4:15   "watch yourselves very carefully"

4:16   "beware lest you act corruptly"

4:19   "beware lest you..."

4:23   "take care, lest you forget"

This section also reminds Israel of the incredible privilege they hold among the nations of the world. God has done the unthinkable in calling them into relationship with him. Note the many references which remind Israel how amazing this covenant relationship with God is:

4:7-8   "For what great nation is there that has a god so near to it as the Lord our God is to us, whenever we call upon him? And what great nation is there, that has statutes and rules so righteous as all this law that I set before you today?

4:20   "But the Lord has taken you and brought you out of the iron furnace, out of Egypt, to be a people of his own inheritance, as you are this day."

4:32   "For ask now of the days that are past, which were before you, since the day that God created man on the earth, and ask from one end of heaven to the other, whether such a great thing as this has ever happened or was ever heard of."

4:33   "Did any people ever hear the voice of a god speaking out of the midst of the fire, as you have heard, and still live?"

4:34   "Or has any god ever attempted to go and take a notion for himself from the midst of another nation, by trials, by signs, by wonders, and by war, by a mighty hand and an outstretched arm, and by great deeds of terror, all of which the Lord your God did for you in Egypt before your eyes?"

As he speaks, Moses reminds the people of who God is. God clearly communicates with his people, he is not fickle, he does not leave Israel guessing at what he wants, and he does not break out against Israel in a tirade for no reason. He is a God like no other. Note the reminders of the person and attributes of God:

4:24 "For the Lord your God is a consuming fire,
    a jealous God."

4:31 "For the Lord your God is a merciful God. He
    will not leave you or destroy you or forget
    the covenant with your fathers that he swore
    them."

4:39 "...the Lord is God in heaven above and on
    the earth beneath; there is no other."

The purpose of this historical reflection is to demonstrate for Israel that they have every reason to trust in God for their future. The God who has been faithful in the past will be faithful in the future. Moses reminds them of this, saying, "To you it was shown, that you might know that the Lord is God; there is no other besides him" (Deuteronomy 4:35). This has been God's primary concern since the beginning of his relationship with the nation, and it is still his primary concern today. He is at work in this world so that we will know who he is and live our lives in humble submission and adoration.

The second sermon (5:1 – 28:68, "The Call to Be God's People") is the central focus of the book. By the end of

Numbers, the entire first generation has perished in the wilderness. So, before Moses dies, he must pass on the covenant stipulations to this second generation and call for their commitment to the covenant before they enter the Promised Land. In reading the Old Testament, this can seem repetitive, but it serves an important purpose. With this section following the historical reflections, we once again see that the call to obedience follows the recognition of God's gracious dealings with his people.

This sermon also presents blessings and curses in chapters 27-28 (these are also taught in Leviticus 26). These passages demonstrate that the Lord longs to bless his people, but the only way the people will experience his blessing is by walking in obedience. True blessing is only found in relationship with one's Creator. And because the Lord loves his people, he will discipline them when they rebel and walk away from him so they feel the pain of separation and return to him. This discipline, therefore, always has restoration of relationship as its goal; and restoration of relationship always results in the return of blessing. Deuteronomy 26:16-19 puts it this way, as a result of obedience "he will set you in praise and in fame and in honor high above all nations that he has made, and that you shall be a people holy to the Lord your God, as he promised." The nation would be set "high above all nations" for praise, fame, and honor. God mercifully makes this as clear as possible. He is a good God.

The third and final sermon (29:1 – 34:12, "Covenant Renewal and Blessing") serves as the book's climax. This sermon is the necessary preliminary step to taking the land. They must give their hearts to the Lord and commit to faithfully follow him so they can conquer the land and occupy their new home. Moses calls them to commit to faithfully following the Lord. Deuteronomy 32:47 states, "For it is no empty word for you, but your very life, and by this word you shall live long in the land that you are going over the Jordan to possess." The goodness of God makes this obedience possible. Deuteronomy 30:11-20 reminds the people that the commandment is "not too hard for you, neither is it far off" (Deuteronomy 30:11). Instead, "the word is very near you. It is in your mouth and in your heart, so that you can do it" (Deuteronomy 30:14). The word is indeed life to them. In giving them the commandments, Moses has "set before you today life and good, death and evil" (Deuteronomy 30:15) and "blessing and curse" (Deuteronomy 30:19). The injunction is to "choose life" (Deuteronomy 30:19).

These are the last words of an old man who knows the Lord, given to a people who need to know him too. Moses has changed. In the beginning, he questioned God over and over as he worked through his doubts and learned to trust him. Several times he went toe-to-toe with the Lord, begging for pardon for the nation. Along the way he knew the pain and consequences of rebellion along with the death and sorrow it brings. And now he clearly offers the words of life to a people who need to hear them. He has truly seen the signs of the most-high God, and he believes in his greatness and his goodness. He knows the Lord is worth following for he alone has the words of life. Time tested. A man of God. This is what God does for those who stay on the path toward him. He changes them and uses them for his glory until he takes them home. Blessed be the name of the Lord.

Context in THE STORY

The book of Deuteronomy does not advance THE STORY; it is just a pause as Moses recounts important concepts to the second generation, post-exodus. Except for Moses, Joshua, and Caleb, the entire first generation has died in the wilderness as a result of their rebellion against the Lord's command to conquer the land. Moses has been denied access to the land and will die before the second generation enters. However, he delivers three important and powerful sermons to this new generation, which has not witnessed all of what the Lord has done for his people since Egypt.

Deuteronomy ends with the people on the plains of Moab just as the book of Numbers ended. THE STORY has not progressed. God has taken time to prepare the nation, and now they are ready. THE STORY continues in the book of Joshua.

Looking Forward to Jesus

The book of Deuteronomy continues the forward movement to Christ. In Deuteronomy 18:15 Moses says, "The Lord your God will raise up for you a prophet like me from among you," which the Lord reiterates in 18:18, "I will raise up for them a prophet like you from among their brothers." In the early days of the New Testament story, the people were looking for the prophet (John 1:21). Additionally, Acts 3:20-24 understands Christ to be the fulfillment of this prophecy (cf. Acts 7:37). But Jesus not only fulfills this promise, he is better than Moses (Hebrews 3:1-5).

CHAPTER THIRTEEN:
THE HISTORICAL BOOKS

As we move into the book of Joshua, we leave behind the Pentateuch and begin a new section known as the Historical Books. The books of the Pentateuch are also historical, but they form their own distinct unit. Even though we are in a new section of the Old Testament, this section picks up THE STORY seamlessly.

Can all of history be trusted? Modern textbooks raise this question, scrutinizing historical information, and rightly so since history is written from a specific cultural perspective, with a particular worldview. In the ancient Near East where the earlier portions of the Old Testament were written, history was generally written with a different focus from that found in the Old Testament. In the ancient Near East, history was written to benefit those in power and cast the best possible light on them. However, in the Old Testament, the purpose is didactic. In other words, history is recorded in order to instruct. More specifically, it is written to carry out the Lord's purposes in this world and to show how the he fulfilled his covenant promises. In one sense, it is a revelation of who the Lord is by recording what he has done. History is simply the record of the Lord carrying out his preordained plans.

Unlike ancient Near Eastern histories, the Old Testament's goal is not to make the powerful look good. In fact, the good, bad, and the ugly are found in these stories. King David is clearly an adulterer who kills one of his trusted friends when it serves his agenda. Even though King Solomon was the wisest man of all time, he failed to heed his own wisdom and turned to idolatrous worship, forsaking the Lord at the end of his life. There is no attempt to make them look better than they were. We see the reality of their lives. Instead, the Old Testament's goal is to let the Lord be seen in all his glory. Neither the actions of King David nor King Solomon are able to thwart the Lord's plans.

Still, with so much history to record, why did the Lord preserve the particular stories found in the Old Testament? To answer this question, we must understand that there are some unique literary features to this new section. Understanding these features will provide insight for grasping the intent of the authors as they write. Since Old Testament history is intended to teach, the authors use patterns and cycles of history. So, understanding the patterns, themes, and motifs is essential to understanding the books that follow. In so doing, the big picture of the Lord's work with his people will become evident. As this happens, our own souls will be transformed.

For instance, in Joshua, two major battles are juxtaposed to teach that obedience brings victory and disobedience brings defeat. In Judges, a repeated cycle highlights Israel's spiritual condition and how it determined her material and political situation. In the books of Samuel and Kings, we see that humanity's failures do not stop the Lord's purposes. The Lord does not demand perfection but rather a repentant heart. Blessing for his people flows from honestly dealing with their sin and turning to him for life. As you read the books, look out for the big picture the author presents.

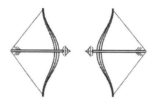

CHAPTER FOURTEEN:
JOSHUA

Joshua picks up THE STORY from the end of Numbers, with the people, who are now the second generation post-exodus, on the plains of Moab, anticipating entering the land. Moses has given them his final words (the three sermons of Deuteronomy) and passed the leadership to Joshua, who will now lead the people into the Promised Land. The conquest and division of the land are in focus. Finally, the promise to Abraham is fulfilled. Finally, God's people have a land of their own.

The meaning of the Hebrew title, Joshua, is "Yahweh is salvation" or "Yahweh saves." Unlike the books of the Pentateuch, the title for this book is not the first word. For the remainder of the books we will study, the name of the book is the same as what we have in our English Bibles.

This book is named for the primary leader, Joshua, who is the most prominent character other than the Lord. He leads the people and provides instructions for everything they are to do.

The author of the book is most likely Joshua himself. The book states clearly that Joshua wrote or had others write certain words in the book (see 8:32; 18:8; 24:26). The use of the first person pronoun, "us," in 5:6 also points to some association with the person Joshua or at least a contemporary. The Jewish Talmud, an important compilation of writings by Jewish scribes, also identifies Joshua as the author. Yet there are many references to things that exist "to this day" (see 4:9; 5:9; 6:25; etc.), which seem to indicate a significant lapse of time from the origination of the event to the time of writing. It very well could have been written during the time of the kingdom (in the books of Samuel and Kings), trying to underscore the importance of obedience to a people who needed to hear that message.

Major Divisions

The book of Joshua is easily divided between chapters 13 and 14. The first part of the book focuses on the actual conquest of the land, including the details of major battles and summaries of major campaigns to take the land. The focus shifts to the distribution of the land in chapter 14. The concerns of the chapters that follow are territories and boundaries for each tribe. Once this is settled, the book ends with a recommitment to follow the ways of the Lord. It is his land and the people are to live under his authority.

Main Message

Some believe that Joshua is a book about a courageous and godly man named Joshua. Although he is a very intriguing man, there is actually very little stated about who this man is. Others summarize the book as a record of military battles. The battle of Jericho is one of the most well-known Bible stories, but apart from this engaging story this book tells very little of military strategy and conquest.

Without a doubt, Joshua is a key figure in Israel's history, although there is not as much written about him as there is for Moses. This is simply a result of the story moving forward more quickly than during Moses' days. Joshua has been by Moses' side for many years, and his name has often appeared in the story, subtly reminding us that he is always close by (see Exodus 17:8-13; 24:13; 32:17). He was recognized as a leader and selected to represent his tribe as one of the 12 spies. Of these 12, he was one of two, the other being Caleb, who gave a good report about the Israelites' ability to conquer the land. This sets him apart as one who, like Caleb, "has a different spirit and has followed [the Lord] fully" (Numbers 14:24). In Numbers 13:16 Moses changes his name from "Hoshea" ("salvation" or "he has delivered") to "Joshua" ("Yahweh saves" or "the Lord has delivered"). There is no reason provided for this change, but it draws attention to Yahweh, the God of Israel, as the deliverer and redeemer of his people. Joshua's legacy is summarized in 24:31: "Israel served the LORD all the days of Joshua, and all the days of the elders who outlived Joshua and had known all the work that the LORD did for Israel."

This book is focused on the victory the Lord provides when the people follow his lead. Here are just a few examples: the Lord tells them when to enter the land (1:1-9), the Lord goes before them to terrify the people of the land (2:9-11), he is "directing the troops" through his captain (5:13-15), he leads them across the Jordan (3-4), he has them circumcised to distinguish them as the people of his covenant (5:1-12), he provides the strategy (6:2-5; 8:2), victory comes from his hand when the people obey him (6:16; 8:7; 10:42), and defeat comes from his hand when they disobey (7:5-12). As we read the book, it becomes clear that the Lord is faithful to his covenant promises and that he is able to bring his people into the land despite the negative report offered by the other ten spies.

The people are to simply follow the leading of the

Lord. They are to be strong and courageous (1:6, 9), which has been the Lord's encouragement throughout Israel's history (Deuteronomy 31:1-13, 14ff, and 27ff). The two battles at the beginning of the book show that the major issue is whether or not the people will be faithful in following the Lord. The battle of Jericho (chapter 6) demonstrates that, despite all apparent odds against Israel or any seemingly ridiculous strategies by the Lord, the people will experience victory as long as they walk in obedience, trusting the Lord's promises. The battle of Ai (chapter 7) demonstrates that, if Israel fails to completely obey the Lord, they will experience the pains of defeat. The juxtaposition of these two chapters provides the clear theology of Joshua: victory belongs to Israel as long as she obeys the Lord.

The sovereign power of the Lord is the reason they are victorious. The Lord is with his people (1:5). With his presence, they can stand against anyone and anything because the Lord is all-powerful. But still the people had been terrified of the inhabitants of the land for many years. In fact, the reason they did not enter the land originally was because they dreaded the "giants" who lived there. In the presence of these giants, they felt like "grasshoppers" (Numbers 13:33) because they forgot the Lord was with them. The truth of God's presence is enough to sustain them through any fears or doubts that arise. The Lord uses the warfare of Israel, but he is the one who brings about their victory.

The Lord is known as the "divine warrior" in the Bible. He is the one who fights for his people as Joshua 10:14 ("for the Lord fought for Israel") and 10:42 ("because the Lord, the God of Israel, fought for Israel") remind us. The Lord fights in a number of ways. Listen to the language of Exodus 23:27-31:

> "I will send my terror before you and will throw into confusion all the people against whom you shall come, and I will make all your enemies turn their backs to you. And I will send hornets before you, which shall drive out the Hivites, the Canaanites, and the Hittites from before you. I will not drive them out from before you in one year, lest the land become desolate and the wild beasts multiply against you. Little by little I will drive them out from before you, until you have increased and possess the land. And I will set your border from the Red Sea to the Sea of the Philistines, and from the wilderness to the Euphrates, for I will give the inhabitants of the land into your hand, and you shall drive them out before you."

The Lord will send his terror, throw the people into confusion, send hornets, and give the inhabitants of the land into the hands of Israel. The Lord also drops hailstones on those who are trying to escape (Joshua 10:11). He is clearly the one who brings victory. The Lord clearly drives out the inhabitants of the land (Exodus 23:27-30). Yet, at the same time, he uses Israel's warfare to accomplish this. The nation of Israel drives them out (Exodus 23:31) and "destroys completely" the inhabitants of the land (Joshua 6:21; 10:35).

That Israel "destroys completely" presents one of the major issues in this book. Also known as "the ban," this practice refers to the consecration of someone's possession for the sanctuary. In war, this means the inhabitants of a city are "set apart" for destruction. Thus, the inhabitants are annihilated or destroyed completely, a practice also found in other ancient near eastern civilizations. God's command for Israel to annihilate the inhabitants of the land is one of the most disturbing realities for those who read the Old Testament.

The legislation for this is found in Deuteronomy 7:1-11 (see also Exodus 23:23; 34:11), and the destruction is aimed at the seven nations that occupied the land Israel was about to enter. Israel is commanded to completely destroy these people. Israel obeys this command in Joshua 6:17-19, 21; 8:1-29; 10:28, 30, 32, 33, 34-35, 37, 39, 40, 41; 11:8, 11, 12, 20-23; and Judges 1:17; the people are at war, but it is the Lord who is the one behind it all (11:18-20). What kind of

God calls for such action?

The Lord provides some reasons if we dig into the Bible a little deeper and give it some thought. The first reason takes us back to Genesis 15:16, where the Lord's promise to Abraham is that his people will one day return to the land and possess it. This land would be what we refer to as the Promised Land, the land of Israel. The Lord does not bring this about quickly for the reason that "the iniquity of the Amorites is not yet complete" (see reason #4 below). However, this promise is fulfilled in the book of Joshua when the people conquer and settle the land.

Second, the Lord desires to protect his people's holiness. In Deuteronomy 7:2-4 we observe that the Lord commands Israel to 1) defeat them, i.e., the Amorites and other "ites" in the land; 2) make no covenant with them, i.e., no offers for peace, only destruction; and 3) not intermarry with them. This is an interesting list of commands if you stop and think about it. If they fulfill the first command and destroy the people, it seems odd to add the other two commands. They would be unnecessary because the people would be dead. The reason is found in verse 4. The Lord's concern is that his people's hearts remain faithful to him and not turn away to serve other gods. This type of rebellion would elicit the Lord's anger, and because he is holy, he would respond by destroying his own people.

To understand the logic of these verses, we must think through the passage backwards, beginning with verse 4 and ending with verse 2. Think of it in this way:

* "Israel, you do not want to fall into the hands of an angry God and be destroyed."

* "Therefore, do not be enticed to turn away and serve other gods."

* "To avoid being vulnerable to this possibility, you are not to intermarry with those of other religions who do not yield their lives to your Lord but rather serve other gods. This will open the door to your destruction."

* "In fact, you are not to even enter into a covenant of peace with this godless people. Make no treaty with them. You are not to be united with them in any way."

* "So, out of my love for you and my desire to preserve your holiness, I command you to destroy them and wipe out any remembrance of the sinful, rebellious ways of their lives. They are an abomination to me. This is for your good and my glory."

Following this kind of reasoning helps us understand the Lord's heart toward his people and toward those who rebel against him. He is seeking to protect his people's holiness.

Third, the Lord is concerned about Israel's vulnerability to deception and idolatry. In this time period people believed that gods ruled over nature and had to be satisfied to avoid serious consequences. Israel was steeped in this worldview. As a result, when Israel encountered difficulty, her natural reaction was to affirm the gods of the particular area. Their thinking was "If we can just make the gods happy, our problems will be solved." This natural reaction is similar to ours when we think, "If I just had more money, my problems would go away." We have a tendency to believe in the "gods" of our world: money, power, and influence. Our worldview similarly impacts the way we think. The Lord knew that these gods would be a temptation to them and could lead them away from him. So, in his mercy, he commands Israel to destroy the people of the land and their gods.

Fourth, the people in the land are wicked. As we saw in Genesis 15:16, the Lord has plans to judge the people of the land. Their wickedness is great, and the Lord must respond to their rebellion. In other words, this people, the Amorites, are a people who are dishonoring the Lord. However, during Abraham's time, the Lord had not yet come to the end of his patience regarding the Amorites' sin. That day would come when the Lord brought Israel back to the land and used them to completely destroy this sinful nation. Note that the Amorites' sins are such an abomination that the Lord will drive Israel out of the land as well if they commit the same sins (Leviticus 18:24-28). In Deuteronomy 7:4, the Lord says he will destroy them if they worship these gods. The Lord is holy, and sin must be judged. So, the Lord uses Israel to execute his judgment against a people who have rejected him and piled sin upon sin. In the process Israel also receives the land promised to them.

The message of the book can be disturbing, confusing, and overwhelming. Yet a careful reading in the context of the bigger story helps us understand the beauty of the Lord's plan. He is advancing his plan and accomplishing his purposes. He is graciously allowing people to turn to him (see the story of Rahab), yet judging those who remain rebellious and refuse to bow to him. His judgment is overwhelmingly painful, but his grace is overwhelmingly good. His judgment makes sense when we properly understand his holiness and majesty. His grace and mercy make no sense, but this is who God is. We must understand the disturbing details of the story in light of the bigger picture. God is amazingly gracious and relentlessly pursues people to redeem them.

Context in THE STORY

The book of Joshua advances THE STORY. Moses is now dead and Joshua is the leader. The second generation, post-exodus, along with Joshua and Caleb, responds to the challenge and faithfully conquers the land that the Lord had promised to Abraham. After the conquest, the tribes receive their inheritance and occupy their territories; then, they renew their commitment to the Lord in a covenant renewal ceremony.

Now that the people are in the Promised Land, what will happen? How will their experience be different? Will they walk in obedience? Will they enjoy the blessings God has promised them? With Joshua's death, THE STORY will continue in the book of Judges. This book will relate to us what happens as the nation begins their new life in the land.

Looking Forward to Jesus

It is exciting to find Israel finally in the land. However, there is more to the story. This land, as good as it is and as much as it has been earnestly desired, is simply a foreshadowing of something better that will be realized through Christ. Even as they desired the Promised Land, they had a greater desire. As Hebrews 11:16 tells us, "But as it is, they desire a better country, that is, a heavenly one. Therefore God is not ashamed to be called their God, for he has prepared for them a city." God continues to make a way, and this way will go through the Messiah, who is still to come.

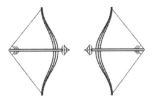

CHAPTER FIFTEEN:
JUDGES

The book of Judges picks up THE STORY from the end of Joshua. The people have finally taken possession of the land promised to Abraham. Joshua faithfully led them throughout the conquest and then divided the land so each tribe had an inheritance. At the end of his life, he initiated a covenant renewal ceremony to encourage the people toward faithfulness. The book ends with his death. Judges picks up THE STORY and describes what life in the land is like.

The meaning of the Hebrew title, Judges, is "Savior" or "Deliver." This is an appropriate title. A focus throughout the book is on the individuals who deliver the Lord's people when their sin brings them into oppressive situations. So, in a sense, the title summarizes the major concern of the book: the Lord raising up individuals to deliver his people. Some judges' heroic feats are described in detail, but others are only summarized. Their actions, once again, display the Lord's grace in dealing with his people.

The author of the book is not identified, but the Jewish Talmud attributes authorship to the prophet and judge, Samuel. 1 Samuel 10:25 refers to a book of writings from the prophet Samuel. This indicates, at least, that Samuel was one who created and preserved historical writings. Similar to the book of Joshua, the message of Judges clearly teaches the nation in Samuel's time about the consequences of disobedience.

Major Divisions

The outline of the book is primarily centered on the various judges, the time of their deliverance, and the nation's subsequent "rest." The book begins by describing how Israel progressed to the state where repeated deliverance was needed and ends with two very descriptive stories demonstrating how bad the situation had become. The basic story is divided into three sections: 1) "The Reason for Israel's Situation," chapters 1-2; 2) "The Story of the Judges," chapters 3-16; and 3) "Two Examples of Depravity," chapters 17-21.

Another way to understand the flow of the book is to

recognize three questions the book asks. Chapters 1-2, and even a part of chapter 3, ask the question "Why does Israel get into such a terrible situation as a nation?" These early chapters explain how the Lord's chosen people made such a mess of living in the land, which was supposed to be a place of blessing for them.

The second question, found in the latter part of chapter 3 through chapter 16, is "What happened to Israel as a result of their failure to maintain covenantal obedience?" This section includes both the consequences of Israel's downfall and the amazing ways the Lord rescues them from their terrible situations. This is the heart of the book—where we see the incredible mercy of the Lord, who continually pursues a people bent on rebelling against him. They hit really low points, but the Lord comes and rescues them from their struggles, wooing them back into relationship, where they can know blessing.

The third question, found in chapters 17-21, is: "How bad did it really get in the days of the judges?" The book of Judges covers many years, so the stories lack certain details. These final chapters demonstrate that the nation had become very wicked in the days of the judges. Reaching back into the stories of the judges (in chapters 3-16) the writer sets forth two examples of Israel's great depravity. It should astound us when we read these two stories that the Lord gave them any opportunities at renewed relationship.

Main Message

Before exploring the main message of the book, it is important to understand how the negative situation developed for Israel. Chapters 1-2 contain the "Why?" question and provide two reasons. Chapter 1 provides the first reason: Israel failed to completely conquer the people in the land of Canaan. The Lord had made it very clear in Deuteronomy 7:2 that they were to completely destroy them. These failures are found in the book of Joshua, but they are very subtly mentioned. Unpacking this issue of failure is not the focus in Joshua, but note the following examples of failure in Joshua that are recounted in Judges 1:

1)   Judges 1:21 – Benjamin is unable to conquer Jerusalem – Joshua 15:63

2)   Judges 1:27-28 – Manasseh is unable to conquer the Canaanites – Joshua 17:11-13

3)   Judges 1:29 – Ephraim is unable to conquer the Canaanites – Joshua 16:10

These examples serve as subtle hints along the way, keeping the narrative historically accurate yet not emphasizing the failure. The old saying, "partial obedience is no obedience," rings true for the nation. They do not fully obey the Lord, and the consequences are devastating.

Chapter 2 provides the second reason: Israel failed to completely destroy the Canaanite religion. Again, Deuteronomy 7:5 clearly stated, "But thus shall you deal with them: you shall break down their altars and dash in pieces their pillars and chop down their Asherim and burn their carved images with fire." Deuteronomy 12:2-3 brings even more force to the command, stating, "You shall surely destroy all the places where the nations whom you shall dispossess served their gods, on the high mountains and on the hills and under every green tree. You shall tear down their altars and dash in pieces their pillars and burn their Asherim with fire. You shall chop down the carved images of their gods and destroy their name out of that place." There was to be no remaining evidence of the gods of the land. Every idol, every place or worship, and every remembrance was to be demolished. Exodus 23:32 points to the heart of the problem: "You shall make no covenant with them and their gods." The issue ultimately was one of heart allegiance. They were to allow no room for any intrusion into their relationship with the Lord. Yet they did, and the consequences are both severe and long-standing.

So the major issues in Judges are mentioned in

Joshua, but they are not explored. They were simply there. Joshua is a triumphant book throughout, so the author does not elaborate on these issues. However, that does not mean they are unimportant. On the contrary, they are very important and even devastating for the nation. The purpose of Judges is to highlight these issues and make it clear that the struggles Israel eventually experiences are the result of her own wrongdoing.

In reflecting on the two reasons above, we must ask why Israel fell away from faith and trust in the Lord so quickly. Two quick points will help us. First, the worship of one god exclusively (monotheism) was not a normal worldview for the culture in which Israel existed. We have touched on this point previously. Suffice it to say that the Israelites struggled with the concept of many gods, and it was natural for them to follow after any god they felt would solve their difficult situation. It is a topic for later, but we will find that we have the same propensity. Second, Israel forgot her history. A strong theme in the book of Deuteronomy is for Israel to remember, not forget (see Deuteronomy 4:9-10, 15, 23; 6:12, 20; 7:17-18; 8:2, 11-20; 9:7; etc.) Deuteronomy 8:11-20 is especially powerful in this regard. They were to remember that the Lord delivered them from Egypt, led them through the wilderness, provided for all their needs as they entered the land (houses they did not build, crops they did not plant, and other blessings), and gave them the land. They were to remember this so they did not become proud and believe they had provided it for themselves by their own power. When we forget the good things the Lord has done for us, we begin to think of ourselves as god. It is a tragedy that leads down the path to death. Israel found herself in that position, so she crowded out the Lord who alone could give her the life and blessings she desired.

We find the main message of the book in chapters 3-16, which contain a repeated cycle. The cycle goes like this: Israel's apostasy, resulting oppression, and God's eventual deliverance through a judge. The repetition drives the author's point home. Israel does not escape this cycle throughout this time period. In fact, it even extends into the books of Samuel, where we find the final cycle before the beginning of the kingdom. Samuel is the final judge, but the nation's deliverance is not found through him. Rather it is secured by Israel's first king, Saul.

Judges 3 serves as a "bridge" between the "Why?" and the "What?" questions. It moves us from the reasons Israel had problems to their actual experience. So, before the cycle is repeated with the various accounts of the judges, it is initially summarized in Judges 3:11-19 with the following steps:

1) Verses 11-13 – Israel did evil in the eyes of the Lord

by following the gods of the land.

2) Verses 14-15 – The Lord raised up enemy nations to oppress Israel. The Lord warned the nation of this consequence in Deuteronomy 28:15ff when he described the curses of covenantal disobedience.

3) Between Verses 15 and 16 – The nation of Israel, who was "severely distressed" by their oppression cried out to the Lord for deliverance.

4) Verse 16-18 – The Lord, in his mercy, answered their cries and raised up a judge to deliver them from their distress. This leads to rest.

5) Verse 19 – The land would be at rest for some years (usually until the judges' death) until, once again, Israel would do evil in the eyes of the Lord by following the gods of the land.

So how bad did it get in Israel during this time? Chapters 17-21 answer this question, providing two snapshots. The first is a picture of Israel's religious degeneration in chapters 17-18: the story of the Danites. This story illustrates how subtle Israel's departure from the Lord could be and how innocent it might have seemed to them. Yet, if we step back and take it all in, this is exactly what the Lord was seeking to prevent. It is an abomination to him. He demands whole-hearted devotion. The second snapshot provides a picture of

Israel's moral degeneration in chapters 19-21: the story of the Benjamites. This is not the kind of story that children's Sunday School stories are made of. This is not how the Lord intends for his people to live. They were to reflect him in all of his glory to the world around them, especially in their relationships with one another. They were to be holy as he is holy.

Judges is written from the perspective of the kingdom. Four times we find the implication that it is written when a king existed (17:6; 18:1; 19:1; 21:25) in the phrase, "In those days there was no king in Israel." Twice the phrase is expanded to, "In those days there was no king in Israel. Everyone did what was right in his own eyes." This addition emphasizes the lack of a Godward focus. Israel needed to see that the lack of blessing they were experiencing was a result of their own failures, not the negligence of the Lord. Consequently, a major purpose in writing the book is to show how Israel's spiritual condition determined its political and material situation. The struggles they encountered while oppressed came because they did not love or obey the Lord.

Whenever Israel gets into trouble, God delivers them through a judge. But what is a "judge?" A quick reading of the book demonstrates that these judges are not necessarily role models or godly examples. They struggle with idolatry, sexual issues, and seem to lack awareness of the Law. Many of these stories of the judges, or at least certain details, will not find their way into children's Sunday School curriculum. Simply put, a judge is a deliverer. The Lord raises up individuals who will bring deliverance. Regardless of what we think of each judge's morality, or lack thereof, we must recognize that their actions were significant. A number of their names are listed in the Hall of Faith in Hebrews 12; in the midst of their corruption, they evidenced faith that is memorialized in this chapter in Hebrews. We must not miss this point as we read their stories and consider their lives.

Once we understand their role, another question surfaces: were they national judges? In other words, did they bring deliverance on a national level? Two issues make it clear that the judges did not function nationally. First, in the phrase, "there was no king in Israel; everyone did what was right in his own eyes," we see that the nation was not united. They are still tribal in nature. Second, there is a chronological problem. If you were to add up all the years of judging along with the years when the nation is at rest, there are too many years for the time period of the judges. 1 Kings 6:1 states that, in the fourth year of Solomon's reign, 480 years had passed since the exodus from Egypt. However, if you add the years represented in the book of Judges, the total is 410. Then, when you add in all of the other years we know of since the exodus, there are too many for the 70 years we have left. Note the following:

*40 years of wilderness wandering

*?? years of settling the land up to Joshua's death

*the years of Samuel's life, the last judge

*the 40 years of King Saul's reign

*the 40 years of King David's reign

TOTAL: 120+ years

So, it is best to understand that the judges delivered the people from local oppression rather than a national one. This means that their judgeships overlapped. Judges 10:7 is probably the best example of this. This verse sets forth two separate oppressions, and the following chapters explain each one as if they were successive, but instead, the oppression and activities of the judges overlapped. It is with King Saul, who acts like a judge in that he brings deliverance, that we finally see a national focus.

Another important question to ask is whether or not we see evidence of true repentance. From the broader biblical story, we know that the escape from sin is repentance. Repentance is TURNING AWAY from sin and idolatry and TURNING TO a life of faith marked by covenant faithfulness flowing from a heart devoted to the

Lord. Consider the following:

*2:4 – "the people lifted up their voices and wept."

*2:17-18 – "the LORD was moved to pity by their groaning

*6:6 – "And Israel was brought very low because of Midian. And the people of Israel cried out for help to the LORD."

*8:23 – "the LORD will rule over you."

*20:1-21:25 – "and the congregation assembled as one man to the LORD at Mizpah." The remainder of the story demonstrates that Israel has turned her heart toward the Lord."

We can probably find other examples, but these show little evidence of repentance. However, regardless of whether or not there is evidence of true repentance, the Lord turns away his wrath and brings rest to the land through the judge. It seems that the Lord is responding to something in the Israelites' hearts. Or is he?

The best example is actually found in 10:10-16. The people recognize their offense to the Lord (v 10). They realize they have TURNED AWAY from the Lord and TURNED TO the Baals, the gods of the Canaanites (v 11). As a result, they put their lives into the Lord's hands (v 15). Some of the language used in this passage casts doubt on their sincerity. For instance, the focus in verse 15 is not ultimately for the Lord to do "whatever." They put a condition on it: "Only please deliver us this day." Also, the decision to "put away the foreign gods from among them" (v 16) is starkly different from the command to obliterate them. This example is as good as it gets. The summation of the Lord's response is "and he became impatient over the misery of Israel" (v 16). This response does not indicate a broken heart.

This apparent lack of repentance is ultimately what makes the message of Judges so powerful. The power is in the contrast between who Israel is and who the Lord is. Israel is rebellious. Israel easily wanders. Israel forgets the good blessings of the Lord. Israel is not even good at repenting. But the Lord is merciful. He pursues. He is gracious. His loving-kindness never fails. His mercy is new every morning. Great is his faithfulness. It is amazing that the Lord continues to be faithful to his covenant despite the people's evil inclinations. He is an amazing God, and that is the story of Judges.

The Book of Ruth

The book of Ruth does not advance THE STORY. The beginning words of the book of Ruth make it clear that this story fits within the period of the judges: "In the days when the judges ruled..." The book does not identify which judge, but this story most likely fits into the early days of the judges. The Bible provides clues to support this. In Ruth 4:21, we learn that Salmon was the father of Boaz. In Matthew 1:5, we learn that Boaz's mother was Rahab (see Joshua 6:25 for the conclusion to her wonderful story). So this story must happen early in the period of the judges. Boaz's mother is alive early in the book of Joshua at the beginning of the conquest. By the time of Joshua's death, her children would have been older, meaning that Boaz probably knew Joshua and the early years in the Promised Land.

The early setting helps us understand the positive nature of this story in contrast to much of what we read in the book of Judges. Israel was faithful throughout Joshua's life, as Joshua 24:31 states, "Israel served the LORD all the days of Joshua, and all the days of the elders who outlived Joshua and had known all the work that the LORD did for Israel." So, by the time of Ruth's story, Israel is not far removed from the covenant faithfulness they experienced after the conquest and throughout Joshua's life. Strong evidence for this is found in the fact that there is still awareness of the Law. In fact, they actually know what the Law teaches and desire to live by it. For example, Boaz could have immediately taken Ruth up on the offer to redeem her, but he knows he must follow the teaching of the Law and that he is not the nearest kin (Ruth 3:12-13).

Others seem to concur with this as the elders convene at the city gate to agree on the right approach to the situation (Ruth 4:1-12). We find another example in the poor who were gleaning in the fields (Ruth 2:2). The Law of Moses made provision for the sojourners, poor, widows, and orphans to gather grain along the borders or corners of the fields or as they walked behind those who were harvesting (Leviticus 19:9-10; 23:22).

As a result, the story of Ruth is in stark contrast to what we read in the rest of Judges. The story reminds us that the Lord will always have a remnant. He will always advance his story, regardless of how evil the nation of Israel might become. So, no matter how bad it gets during the time of the judges, the Lord will continue to advance his plans, especially concerning the redemption of his people through the coming Messiah. This is evident not only by the story itself, but by the genealogy that ends the book. This genealogy tells us that King David is descended from Ruth, and as THE STORY reveals, the Messiah is descended from King David. The Lord will make a way. His plans will move forward.

Context in THE STORY

The book of Judges clearly advances THE STORY, moving the reader from the conquest and settling of the land to the majesty and turmoil of the kingdom period to follow. Israel's occupation of the land is fraught with difficulty, but the Lord faithfully maintains his covenant and provides Israel with continual opportunities to turn back to him so they can know the blessings that flow from properly worshipping his name. The book of Ruth does not advance THE STORY; instead it is an additional story of what happened during the days of the Judges, demonstrating that the Lord is advancing his purposes despite the mess his people make of life in the Promised Land. The Lord continues to work with a remnant, and he will raise up the Deliverer.

1 and 2 Samuel will pick up THE STORY. As we open the pages of these books, we will still be in the time period of the judges. The cycle continues. Israel turns away. But the Lord will be faithfully living out the covenant.

Looking Forward to Jesus

When we consider how this book points to the coming of Jesus, we probably think about how the people are not experiencing the blessings of being in the land. In other words, if this is all there is, the people of God are in trouble. They are not doing a very good job of following their Lord; consequently, they experience much more curse than blessing. The story of Judges emphasizes that sin is a problem which must be overcome. The people's hearts are easily and continuously turned away. There is much pain and suffering to endure. There must be more, and that "more" will be found in Jesus and Jesus alone. Judges reminds us that our hope must be found apart from humanity and the law. As the old hymn states, "My hope is built on nothing less than Jesus' blood and righteousness; I dare not trust the sweetest frame, but wholly lean on Jesus' name." Thank you, Jesus.

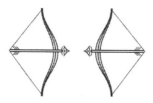

CHAPTER SIXTEEN:
THEOLOGY OF JOSHUA AND JUDGES

The books of Joshua and Judges (along with Ruth) serve as a mini-unit in the Historical Books. There is a natural connection between the stories as this is the time period between the life of Moses and the kingdom. So, as we come to the theology, it is natural to think through the message of these books together. Understanding the manner in which the authors were writing makes the theological point is most clear. In the chapter on "The Historical Books" we established that in writing these histories the author emphasized cycles to make his point. Now, I want to turn our attention to how these books affect our contemporary situation.

The books teach that those who seek relationship with the Lord and follow his design for life wholeheartedly will know the blessings that flow from knowing him. Joshua establishes the foundation for this principle as it sets forth the two battles at the beginning of the book. Jericho stands as an example of the blessings that flow from following the Lord's instructions no matter how bizarre they might be. Ai demonstrates that the slightest deviation from the Lord's commands, coupled with the desire to find life in one's own way, will lead to disastrous consequences. Judges continues this teaching. The people are now in the land, but this does not guarantee the blessing of the Lord. The Lord wants to bless his people, but they must obey him if they are to know the kind of life and blessing they desire. This will only be found in the Lord and by walking in his ways. So, when the people walk away from the Law of the Lord, they experience the devastation that results from their choices. In both books, the nation experiences the discipline of the Lord through difficulty, but the difficulty is ultimately for their good. The Lord is seeking to draw them back to him so they can know the blessings he longs to give them.

Maintaining obedience to the Mosaic Law is central from the first chapter of Joshua. Chapter 1, verses 5-9 state:

No man shall be able to stand before you all the days of your life. Just as I was with Moses, so I will be with you. I will not leave you or forsake you. Be strong and courageous, for you shall cause this people to inherit the land that I swore to their fathers to give them. Only be strong and very courageous, being careful to do according to all the law that Moses my servant commanded you. Do not turn from it to the right hand or to the left, that you may have good success wherever you go. This Book of the Law shall not depart from your mouth, but you shall meditate on it day and night, so that you may be careful to do according to all that is written in it. For then you will make your way prosperous, and then you will have good success. Have I not commanded you? Be strong and courageous. Do not be frightened, and do not be dismayed, for the LORD your God is with you wherever you go.

What is the key to a blessed life? Knowing, understanding, and obeying the word of the Lord, which invites us to live the life that is found only in him.

And it is not simply the word of the Lord. The work of the Lord is also vital (refer to the Theology of Numbers). We are to develop a storehouse of memories of what the Lord has done so that we might trust him in the unknown. He has not only said that he alone is the path to life, he has proven it by his actions. So, in Joshua 4, he reminds the Israelites one more time who he is by demonstrating his power through his works. Miraculously, he dries up the waters of the Jordan River so the people walk through on dry ground. The nation then sets up stones to serve as a reminder of what the Lord had done. Joshua 4:21-24 states:

> And he said to the people of Israel, "When your children ask their fathers in times to come, 'What do these stones mean?' then you shall let your children know, 'Israel passed over this Jordan on dry ground.' For the LORD your God dried up the waters of the Jordan for you until you passed over, as the LORD your God did to the Red Sea, which he dried up for us until we passed over, so that all the peoples of the earth may know that the hand of the LORD is mighty, that you may fear the LORD your God forever."

The Lord has the power to do whatever he wants, and Israel needs to trust in him alone, including everything he reveals to them in his word.

In Joshua 6:2, when the Lord says, "See, I have given Jericho into your hand, with its king and mighty men of valor," Israel's response should be to trust him and do whatever he calls them to do. He is the Lord, and he is trustworthy. In Joshua 6:3-20a, the Lord tells the people what to do. The story does not mention it, but what the Lord is asking his people to do is quite ridiculous considering they are in a war. Nonetheless, they do it, and they should. The Lord has proven himself trustworthy, and his word should be trusted and followed. The result found in Joshua 6:20b-27 is Israel's victory. As Israel obeys the Lord, the Lord accomplishes what he said he would do. Once again, he proves he is to be trusted, and that life is found in obedience to him.

This simple point is made throughout the Bible and most Christians can understand and articulate it. However, it is easy for us to neglect the call to wholeheartedly follow the Lord because of the competing voices that call for our attention. Psalm 1 drives this point home. It contrasts two ways of living: the evil man and the blessed man. Let me explain this a little so that you can understand this psalm and connect it to your life.

Psalm 1 is a comparison of two choices which result in either the blessed life or the wicked life. The psalm seeks to underscore what it is that makes a man blessed. The Hebrews communicated their thoughts in a particular way. In poetry they utilized the symmetry of ideas, which were grouped in chiasms, or pairs. In other words, these pairs were arranged according to ideas. In Psalm 1, consider this arrangement of the psalm and the similar ideas of the pairs:

1 – Present Life Experience of the Blessed Man, v 1

2 – The Focus on the Torah, v 2

3 – Comparison for the blessed man, v 3

3 – Comparison for the wicked ones, v 4

2 – [?????????????????]

1 – Future Life Experience of the Wicked Ones, vv 5-6

You can see the connections of ideas represented by the numbers 1, 2, and 3. The point in the psalm is made by what is missing. See the question marks? For the wicked ones, there is no "paired" or similar idea concerning the focus on the Torah, which is present for the blessed man. In other words, the wicked ones do not focus on the Torah, which leads to empty lives and ultimately results in death or separation from the Lord. Psalm 1 makes it clear that the wise way to live is by bringing the Torah into one's life. This leads to blessing. Matthew 7 makes the same point with the parable of the two foundations. The wise man builds his foundation on the words of Jesus so he can make it through the unavoidable storms of life. This, too, leads to blessing.

Again, this is the point Joshua and Judges are trying to make. Obedience results in blessing. Additionally, the books teach that the Lord will do whatever he can to bring people to the end of themselves so they turn back to him and live. Why? Life is found in listening to and obeying the Lord because of who he shows himself to be. This is true for us as well. Here is the pattern:

1) The Lord gives his people revelation that shows them how to live so they can know the life that he freely offers to those who faithfully follow him.

2) When the Lord's people fall away and rebel, the Lord offers the opportunity for repentance and forgiveness, leading to restored relationship with him. People can come back to him and enjoy relationship once again.

3) Even when the Lord's people stubbornly refuse to turn back to the Lord, he pursues and does whatever it takes to bring them to their end, giving them every opportunity to return. Throughout the Bible, the Lord uses difficulty to bring people to a vulnerable place so that turning to any option apart from him becomes futile. He becomes the only option. This is why the New Testament calls difficulty good.

4) The difficulties of life are ultimately the mercy of the Lord as he uses difficulty to drive people back to him because life is only found in him.

The point of difficulty is the same throughout the Bible, from Adam and Eve to the nation of Israel. It is also true for our lives today.

Like Israel, we fail. We stubbornly turn away. Immaturity is present in each of us, and we need to be growing daily. But, when we do fail, the Lord in his mercy may bring difficulty into our lives as well. The goal of this difficulty will be the same for us as it was for Israel. The Lord is bringing us to an end of ourselves so we will turn back to him. So, we repent and turn back. Then we fail and repent and turn back. Again, we fail. Again, we repent and turn back. This is the Christian life. Failure is not the problem. The problem is refusing to repent and turn back. The Lord is faithful and good, and he is waiting to receive us back into fellowship with him. This is why he is doing everything he can to bring us to the end of ourselves.

Let us look to the Lord alone for life. The only way we can do this is to know his word and prayerfully seek to live it day by day. We are sure to fail because we are sinners, but we are washed in the blood of Jesus. So we face our sin honestly, repent, and turn back to the Lord. Israel stubbornly fought against the Lord, and so can we. However, there is another path. He alone is life. Let's look to him.

Making It Real

1)   Although it is difficult to know with certainty, might you be experiencing discipline presently in your life? Think about the goodness of this difficulty. Let it stir your

heart toward the Lord that you might love him more and follow him more fully.

2)   Do you have a tendency to relax your relationship with the Lord when life is going good for you? Do you become satisfied with his goodness and begin taking him for granted? If you are like most people throughout the generations, then you have experienced or are experiencing this to some degree. Why do you think this is true? How does this attitude lead to an eventual turning away from the Lord in some type of rebellion?

3)   It is debatable whether or not Israel truly experienced repentance. What is true repentance? Simply put, it is TURNING AWAY from that which is displeasing to the Lord and TURNING TOWARD that which is pleasing to him. Do you experience this in your own life? Do you need to seek the Lord in repentance now? Spend some time in confession right now and give your life to the Lord afresh.

4)   Standing back, it is easy to see how stupid it was for Israel to continually turn away from the Lord. The only time they experienced his rest was when they actively sought him with their whole heart. Consider you or your friends for a moment; is your life any different? Do you also experience ups and downs in your relationship with the Lord? What is the antidote for this? Hint: they needed to know the Torah and live the Torah to know the blessing of life in the land. How does this translate into your life?

CHAPTER SEVENTEEN:
1 AND 2 SAMUEL

The book of Joshua gives us the story of Israel conquering and settling the Promised Land. The book of Judges provides us a glimpse into the first stage of the nation's occupation of the land. The books of 1 and 2 Samuel now pick up THE STORY, and we see the Lord take the nation to the next level so to speak. Israel has struggled with obedience, yet the Lord continues to advance his plans by transitioning them from judges to the kingdom, setting the stage for the coming of the Messianic King.

The title of the book, Samuel, means "God has heard." It is named after the person responsible for moving the nation from the judges to the kingdom. Samuel was named because God heard the cry of Hannah's heart (1

Samuel 1:20). There is no mention of authorship in the book. The Jewish Talmud (again, this is a commentary from the rabbis) ascribes authorship to Samuel, Nathan, and Gad. This is based on 1 Chronicles 29:29-30, which states, "Now the acts of King David, from first to last, are written in the Chronicles of Samuel the seer, and in the Chronicles of Nathan the prophet, and in the Chronicles of Gad the seer, with accounts of all his rule and his might and of the circumstances that came upon him and upon Israel and upon all the kingdoms of the countries." In our discussion in the book of Judges we also noted 1 Samuel 10:25 and the reference to Samuel compiling historical documents for the nation. However, there is no clear evidence as to who wrote these books or 1 and 2 Kings.

As we enter the books of Samuel, the time in the Promised Land for the Lord's people has been marked less by blessing and more by struggle. Obedience to the Mosaic Law has not been easy for them. However, the Lord has demonstrated two significant realities. First, blessing is possible because he is merciful. The nation should have learned that no matter how bad their rebellion might be or how many times they might walk away and return, the Lord is merciful and offers renewed relationship. He is waiting, and he even longs for them to return so he can bless them. Second, the sin of the nation is not going to stop the Lord's plans to redeem them. He will make a way.

No matter how rampant rebellion is, the Lord preserves a remnant who are willing to bow to him. No matter how often the people turn away, the Lord continues to stir hearts and draw people to himself so he can accomplish his purposes. One thing is clear: the nation has no reason to boast in themselves. Anything of value they have received has been given to them by the Lord. As such, all boasting goes to him.

We now enter the kingdom period. The Lord is going to do something new with his people in the books of Samuel and Kings. There is a unity to these books. In the Greek translation, known as the Septuagint, the books of Samuel and Kings are even referred to as the four books of kings. However, as we open to Samuel, we are still in the period of the judges. The cycle is repeating. Note 1 Samuel 12:6-12:

And Samuel said to the people, "The LORD is witness, who appointed Moses and Aaron and brought your fathers up out of the land of Egypt. Now therefore stand still that I may plead with you before the LORD concerning all the righteous deeds of the LORD that he performed for you and for your fathers. When Jacob went into Egypt, and the Egyptians oppressed them, then your fathers cried out to the LORD and the LORD sent Moses and Aaron, who brought your fathers out of Egypt and made them dwell in this place. But they forgot the LORD their God. And he sold them into the hand of Sisera, commander of the army of Hazor, and into the hand of the Philistines, and into the hand of the king of Moab. And they fought against them. And they cried out to the LORD and said, 'We have sinned, because we have forsaken the LORD and have served the Baals and the Ashtaroth. But now deliver us out of the hand of our enemies, that we may serve you.' And the LORD sent Jerubbaal and Barak and Jephthah and Samuel and delivered you out of the hand of your enemies on every side, and you lived in safety. And when you saw that Nahash the king of the Ammonites came against you, you said to me, 'No, but a king shall reign over us,' when the LORD your God was your king."

Once again, similar to the period of the judges, we find an enemy nation oppressing Israel. The nation must learn the simple lesson that life is not found in turning away from the Lord; it is only found in the Lord. Samuel pleads with the people in verses 14 and 15 saying, "If you will fear the LORD and serve him and obey his voice and not rebel against the commandment of the LORD, and if both you and the king who reigns over you will follow the LORD your God, it will be well. But if you will not obey the voice of the LORD, but rebel against the commandment of the LORD, then the hand of the LORD will be against you and your king." Obedience is the only way to break the cycle of rebellion. Now, as we move into the period of the kingdom, the king becomes the person responsible for leading the people to the Lord. This has been the plan since the responsibilities of the king were given in Deuteronomy 17:14-20. The king must know the Law and lead the nation in obedience. It is the only way to break the cycle that has dominated the nation for years.

Major Divisions

There are four major divisions to the book. The life of David spills over into the books of Kings, so it is awkward to only provide an outline for the books of Samuel. That is a good reason to view the four books as a unit. However, for our purposes here, let's use the following as our guide:

I. 1 Samuel 1 – 1 Samuel 7: The Transition from Judge to King: The Leadership of Samuel

II. 1 Samuel 8 – 1 Samuel 15: Israel's First King: The Rise and Fall of King Saul

III. 1 Samuel 16 – 2 Samuel 2:4: The Struggle Between Kings: The Rise of King David

IV. 2 Samuel 2:5 – 2 Samuel 20: Israel's Greatest King: The Reign of King David

Section one moves the narrative from the judges to the kingdom. Samuel is both a judge and a priest. His godly leadership helps Israel avoid more oppression and remain focused on the Lord.

Section two initiates the kingdom. Saul is the first king, but he functions like a judge. To clarify, the focus of his reign is on delivering and uniting the kingdom. He brings the 12 tribes together under his leadership, and for the first time since the nation entered the land, there is a national focus.

Section three is probably the strangest part of the book. In these chapters, we see a struggle between the anointed king, David, and the reigning king, Saul. Saul's heart in these chapters is ugly, which magnifies the heart of David as a man and king after God's own heart. Even an evil king cannot stop the purposes of the Lord. He will make a way to advance his plans and accomplish his purposes.

Section four gives us the reign of King David. He establishes the pattern of what it means to be a good king, who is after the heart of the Lord. His obedience, and even his repentance when he is disobedient, provides future kings with a model to follow. Any good king in Israel's future is referred to as a "king like David."

Main Message

This is not a historical book in the strictest sense. As with all of the historical books, the theological emphasis is the essential focus. The Lord is advancing his plans. His covenant program continues to unfold in these books, which provide the details of the Davidic Covenant. The books also provide a proper concept of divine authority. The Lord must be acknowledged as the sovereign one advancing his plans. The star of the story is not any of the individuals at the center of the developing nation. The power and influence these individuals possess is not the result of their upbringing or natural abilities. The success they experience is not derived from their prowess or quick thinking. Success is experienced only through the goodness of the Lord. The Lord is the star of this story! He is the one who is enthroned in the heavens with the earth as his footstool. It is he who establishes the Davidic Covenant in his time and in his way. He is the ultimate King. If a king does not follow the Lord, then he is removed (i.e., Saul, 1 Samuel 15:26-31)) or encounters the discipline of the Lord (i.e., David, 2 Samuel 12:9-12). This simple theological point—that the Lord is sovereign overall and is working out his plans in this world—is the only reason Israel experiences any success.

The early part of the book provides a glimpse into the hearts of the Israelite people. In these early chapters, we are obviously still in the time of the judges and Israel is at a low point, experiencing another cycle of rebellion against the Lord. This is especially true as the author examines the condition of the priests: "Now the sons of Eli were worthless men. They did not know the LORD" (1 Samuel 2:12). The spiritual leaders do not know the Lord! 1 Samuel 2:17 reveals the extent of their rebellion: "Thus the sin of the young men was very great in the sight of the LORD, for the men treated the offering of the LORD with contempt." This careless, dishonoring attitude reveals that their hearts are not oriented toward the Lord. This lack of honor for the Lord is then contrasted with the Philistines' recognition of the Lord's greatness in 1 Samuel 5, even though they do not properly acknowledge the person of the Lord. The Philistines steal the Ark of the Covenant and bring it to their own house of worship, the temple of Dagon. 1 Samuel 5:2-5 reads:

Then the Philistines took the ark of God and brought it into the house of Dagon and set it up beside Dagon. And when the people of Ashdod rose early the next day, behold, Dagon had fallen face downward on the ground before the ark of the LORD. So they took Dagon and put him back in his place. But when they rose early on the next morning, behold, Dagon had fallen face downward on the ground before the ark of the LORD, and the head of Dagon and both his hands were lying cut off on the threshold. Only the trunk of Dagon was left to him.

The Philistines clearly see that the Lord is to be feared for he is great and powerful, and they acknowledge him as such. Yet, they do not bow to him; instead they send him away, preferring their own gods, who cannot even stand against him. This is one of several examples in the Old Testament where the people of pagan nations are given every opportunity to bow before the Lord, yet they reject him in all his glory. But the contrast is still interesting to note. Israel sees the Lord as not able to protect them from the Philistines. The Philistines acknowledge the great power of the Lord, yet they send him away. This sets the stage for Israel's request for a king.

Kingship is central to this book. The promise of a king is found early in Israel's story, Genesis 17:6, 16 and 35:11 give hints of a day when a king would reign over the Lord's people. Genesis 49:10 also points to the king coming from Judah. Deuteronomy 17:14-20 established the guidelines for a king as Moses anticipated the day when a king would reign in Israel. In the book of Judges, we find more anticipation for the coming of a king (8:22-23; 9:1-2). Finally, in the books of Samuel this anticipation is fulfilled.

Even though this day is anticipated, the story in Samuel implies that the desire for a king is a wrong one. 1 Samuel 8:4-9 reads:

Then all the elders of Israel gathered together and came to Samuel at Ramah and said to him, "Behold, you are old and your sons do not walk in your ways. Now appoint for us a king to judge us like all the nations." But the thing displeased Samuel when they said, "Give us a king to judge us." And Samuel prayed to the LORD. And the LORD said to Samuel, "Obey the voice of the people in all that they say to you, for they have not rejected you, but they have rejected me from being king over them. According to all the deeds that they have done, from the day I brought them up out of Egypt even to this day, forsaking me and serving other gods, so they are also doing to you. Now then, obey their voice; only you shall solemnly warn them and show them the ways of the king who shall reign over them."

Samuel is displeased. The Lord says they have rejected him as King. This seems disconnected from the many passages that point to a coming king. This presents a problem. However, the problem is not their desire for a king, but rather that they ask for the wrong reasons. They believe a king will succeed where God had "failed." A king would come, but at this point, the nation is moving contrary to the Lord and trying to establish by human effort something only the Lord was to do. They are turning away from him and his lead in an effort to fix their situation in their own way. They want a king like the nations around them (cf. 1 Samuel 8:5; 12:12). They believe this king will be their deliverer. 1 Samuel 10:19 reads, "But today you have rejected your God, who saves you from all your calamities and your distresses, and you have said to him, 'Set a king over us.'" They rejected the only one who could save them and turned to one who was powerless to save them apart from the Lord. They failed to see that their oppression is a result of their sin, not the failure of the Lord. The Lord has been faithful to them, even after they have continually been unfaithful. Israel's request for a king is a rejection of their true king, the Lord.

The books focus on the lives of Samuel, Saul, and David. As has been mentioned, Samuel transitions the nation to the kingdom, moving them out of the time of the judges, and serves as their spiritual advisor during this time. During his life, the focus shifts to the two kings. The difference between the two kings can almost be summed up in their selection. Note the description of Saul in 1 Samuel 9:2, "And he had a son whose name was Saul, a handsome young man. There was not a man among the people of Israel more handsome than he. From his shoulders upward he was taller than any of the people." Also, 1 Samuel 10:23-24 states, "And when he stood among the people, he was taller than any of the people from his shoulders upward. And Samuel said to all the people, 'Do you see him whom the LORD has chosen? There is none like him among all the people.' And all the people shouted, 'Long live the king!'" The emphasis for King Saul is his outward appearance. The people wanted a deliverer, one different from the Lord. As they looked at their new king, it was obvious that he could lead them to battle and accomplish great victory. In the end they got a king who lacked spiritual awareness. He does not seem to know who Samuel is (1 Samuel 9:10—15). He does not understand the seriousness of his offenses in offering the sacrifice (1 Samuel 13:8-12), failing to execute Agag and destroy the spoil (1 Samuel 15:13-35), and using divination to gain information (1 Samuel 28:6-7). All of this adds up to a strong deliverer, but one who is not spiritually focused.

King David is described very differently. As Samuel was seeking to anoint the next king, the Lord gives him this directive in 1 Samuel 16:7, "When they came, he looked on Eliab and thought, 'Surely the LORD's anointed is before him.' But the LORD said to Samuel, 'Do not look on his appearance or on the height of his stature, because I have rejected him. For the LORD sees not as man sees:

man looks on the outward appearance, but the LORD looks on the heart.'" The people had run ahead of the Lord and found their own king, King Saul. He was their outward-appearance king. The Lord had enough of that. He informs Samuel that he is looking at the heart. In the Lord's plan, the king will be of a different stature with an inward focus on his heart. When David shows up, 1 Samuel 16:12 says "he was ruddy and had beautiful eyes and was handsome. And the LORD said, 'Arise, anoint him, for this is he.'" He was just a good-looking guy. There is no fanfare. The Lord simply says to anoint him.

The story that follows demonstrates the contrast between the two kings. King Saul is a power-hungry, arrogant, and evil man. Whereas David, who has not officially been given the kingdom, is a humble, courageous, and God-fearing man, who can be trusted to shepherd the Lord's people. King Saul repeatedly attempts to murder David. Whereas David has the opportunity to take King Saul's life twice (1 Samuel 24 and 26), yet chooses to entrust himself to the Lord and wait for him to provide the throne. David is continually affirmed as a man after God's own heart, and his destiny to be king is celebrated (1 Samuel 16:12-13; 19:4-5; 24:16-22). Stories are never simply historical. There is always a theological point. The theological point in this instance is that the Lord is the one who puts David on the throne; David does not take the kingdom that is rightfully his. This is a beautiful picture of what it means to wait on the Lord.

Finally, in 2 Samuel 2:4, David assumes the throne and has his own share of problems throughout his life and reign. The multiplication of wives (2 Samuel 5:13) is a direct violation of the call to kingship found in Deuteronomy 17:17. His sin with Bathsheba (2 Samuel 11), which was ultimately an abuse of power, and her resulting pregnancy was not pleasing to the Lord and had horrible repercussions on his family (2 Samuel 12). Additionally, this sin led to the murder of Uriah, one of his mighty men, after repeated attempts to cover up Bathsheba's pregnancy, and, finally, the seeming pride of King David's census toward the end of his life (2 Samuel 24). However, even though we clearly see King David's sins, more importantly, we see his humble heart of repentance when he is confronted. This is what it means to be a man after God's own heart.

The Davidic Covenant

A major focus in the book is the Davidic Covenant. We already discussed this in a previous chapter, but now we can reemphasize this covenant in its historic context. This covenant serves as the central point of Samuel. It is found in 2 Samuel 7:16, which reads, "And your house and your kingdom shall be made sure forever before me. Your throne shall be established forever." Remember, each covenant has a promise and an obligation. The obligation of this covenant is continued faithfulness to the Mosaic Covenant and its law. However, this obligation only brings about temporary blessings on the nation as a king obeys the Mosaic Law and calls the nation to obedience as well. The principle of the Davidic Covenant is this:

If a king was obedient to the Mosaic Law by worshipping the Lord exclusively, desiring to live out the law and love one's neighbor in a way that honored the Lord, and perpetuating the covenant to each generation, then the nation would be blessed and would know peace and rest from their enemies, prosperity in their work, and the expansion of their borders. However, if a king was disobedient to the Mosaic Law by worshipping other gods, not living out the law in a manner that honored one's neighbor, and disregarding the perpetuation of the covenant to future generations, then the nation would be judged and would know defeat and oppression from their enemies, failure and difficulty in their work, and ultimately exile into foreign lands.

As long as a king lived obediently and led the nation in obedience, then the Promised Land would be what it was promised to be, a land flowing with milk and honey. However, if the covenant was not kept by the king or by the nation, the consequences would only be temporary. The promise of this covenant is much bigger than Israel's ability to keep her end of the deal. The Lord will ensure the fulfillment of this covenant promise. This covenant is Messianic, meaning that it will find its ultimate fulfillment, not in an earthly king, but rather in Jesus Christ. The Lord will make a way. He is advancing his purposes in the world through the nation of Israel, despite any rebellion on their part. The Lord will be faithful to redeem a people for himself, ultimately from all over the world.

Context in THE STORY

The books of Samuel clearly pick up THE STORY from the book of Judges, and, in fact, as these books begin, we are still in the time of the judges. Samuel is the one who brings about the transition to the kingdom as he anoints the first two kings. The books of Samuel tell THE STORY of the nation during this time. THE STORY will be picked up by the books of Kings, where we will learn more about what God is doing, how the nation is responding, and who God uses to move THE STORY along and accomplish his purposes.

Looking Forward to Jesus

In the books of Samuel the movement toward Jesus gains momentum. In 1 Samuel 2:1-10, we read Hannah's amazing prayer to the Lord concerning his greatness, his person, and his work. In verses 9-10, the Messiah is in view: "He will guard the feet of his faithful ones, but the wicked shall be cut off in darkness, for not by might shall a main prevail. The adversaries of the Lord shall be broken to pieces; against them he will thunder in heaven. The Lord will judge the ends of the earth; he will give strength to his king and exalt the horn of his anointed." "His anointed" is best translated as "his Messiah." This is the first use of the term in the Bible, anticipating the day when this Messiah will be exalted and usher in his kingdom, where the evil are punished and the righteous protected.

Also, 1 Samuel 2:35-36 could be a reference to the coming Messiah, continuing the prediction of Deuteronomy 18:15 and 18. This passage anticipates a "faithful priest, who shall do according to what is in my heart and mind forever." Although there is a more immediate fulfillment in Zadok, it also points forward as this priest is believed to "go in and out before my anointed forever" (verse 35). The book of Hebrews points to the supremacy of the faithfulness of Jesus, our High Priest (Hebrews 4:16-5:10).

The Davidic Covenant in 2 Samuel 7:12-16 clearly points to the one who is coming. This promised king will have a forever throne (verses 13 and 16). This is fulfilled in Christ, the Messiah. It is his kingdom that will last forever. All of the Old Testament begins to look forward to this day from this moment on. The Messiah will first come to give his life as a ransom for many, because sinful people need atonement, then he will return to usher in his kingdom.

CHAPTER EIGHTEEN:
THEOLOGY OF 1 AND 2 SAMUEL

The theological focus in this chapter actually involves the first few chapters of 1 Kings because it flows from a comparison of the three major kings of Israel: Kings Saul, David, and Solomon. From the stories of these three kings we find two related theological points. First, the success of God's people is directly related to how they relate with him. If he is honored as his nature requires, the people will know blessing. On the other hand, if he is not honored, the people will know the consequences of their disobedience. Second, these stories display the Lord's loving-kindness to those who turn from their sin and turn to him in repentance, seeking his face.

Addressing the first theological point requires that we look at the lives of these three kings. Their lives follow a similar pattern. There is a rise to greatness, a turning point involving sin, and a fall from the Lord's favor. In the first phase of this pattern, the story focuses on the successes of the kings, which are many. In the second phase, the story focuses on a major failure in the life of the king. In each account emphasis is given to the king's response when admonished by the Lord. The way each king responds to the Lord's pursuit of his heart is directly related to the severity of the consequences. In the final phase of this pattern, the story focuses on the devastating consequences of the king's actions. To make this pattern clear, let us look at the life of each king.

King Saul

For King Saul, the first phase is most apparent in his army's many conquests against the foes of Israel. Up to this point in the story, Israel has been tribal and, as a result, not able to solidify its standing against the surrounding nations. King Saul unifies the tribes and provides leadership to a nation, not just separate tribes. With their united efforts and the Lord's blessing, they slowly defeat their enemies, bringing unprecedented peace to the nation. For the first time, God's people look like what we would expect from a people who know the One True God. The nation is in the land, and they are enjoying the Lord's blessings. They are at peace and are thriving under their new leadership.

The turning point for Saul is found in 1 Samuel 13 and 15. In chapter 13, Saul assumes the role of priest and offers a sacrifice because the real priest, Samuel, was delayed. Saul felt anxious as he saw the Philistine army gathered around him. Lacking trust in his faithful Lord, who had given him all things, he hastily offers the sacrifice. This move exposes either his lack of understanding of, or his clear disregard for, the teaching of the Law concerning the offer of sacrifice. Deuteronomy 17 clearly shows that the king was to lead people in obedience to the Law, not publicly disregarded the Law's mandates. Then, in 1 Samuel 15, Saul does not fully obey the Lord and devote the Amalekites, both humans and animals, to the ban (to destruction). Instead, he disregards the Lord's instructions and preserves Agag and the animals perceived to be "good." Once again, rather than lead the people in obedience, he publicly disregards the word of the Lord and does as he pleases. In both instances, King Saul is confronted and given opportunity to respond. In both cases, he fails to respond in a manner that honors the Lord. He shifts blame (1 Samuel 15:21), rationalizes his actions (1 Samuel 13:11-12; 15:15, 24), and minimizes his disobedience (1 Samuel 15:25). Rather than own his sinfulness and seek the Lord's forgiveness, he seeks to make himself look good.

The final phase, the fall, occurs shortly after these two scenes. 1 Samuel 15:10-11 tell us, "The word of the LORD came to Samuel: 'I regret that I have made Saul king, for he has turned back from following me and has not performed my commandments.'" After a weak attempt by King Saul to appease the prophet, Samuel responds in 1 Samuel 15:26-29, saying,

> "[For] you have rejected the word of the LORD, and the LORD has rejected you from being king over Israel." As Samuel turned to go away, Saul seized the skirt of his robe, and it tore. And Samuel said to him, "The LORD has torn the kingdom of Israel from you this day and has given it to a neighbor of yours, who is better than you. And also the Glory of Israel will not lie or have regret, for he is not a man, that he should have regret."

The fall is abrupt, quick, and total. King Saul has no future. The Lord will be obeyed and honored or there will be consequences to his people.

King David

King David's rise begins early in Saul's reign as their lives are contrasted in 1 Samuel 16-31. Saul has already "fallen," so David's rise begins before he even takes the throne. He is anointed, but for many years he serves his Lord while he waits to assume the throne that is rightfully his. As a result, his rise is demonstrated initially and primarily by his character and then eventually by his conquests. King Saul, after his fall, is depicted as a man who is wholly self-focused, seeking to preserve whatever semblance of self-perceived respect he might have. His jealousy is so great that on two occasions, he seeks to take David's life. Yet David, who is a man of high character, seeks to honor King Saul because he is the Lord's anointed. Even though he is intentionally and evilly denigrated, he seeks to serve Saul and preserve the people's allegiance to him. King David is on the rise. His life speaks for itself. In addition, when David assumes the throne, he continues the nation's dominance of surrounding nations, defeating foes and expanding the borders. Peace and prosperity abound during his reign. The Lord even enters into a covenant relationship with King David (the Davidic Covenant in 2 Samuel 7), making him the most prominent king of all time, the predecessor of the Messiah.

The turning point for King David comes in 2 Samuel 11. In lust King David commits adultery, which was clearly prohibited for a king in Deuteronomy 17. The king was not allowed to add wives because it would be an abuse of power. 2 Samuel 7 demonstrates this. King David violates

Bathsheba because he can. He is the king. He can take whatever he wants, and he does. His lust remains secret until Bathsheba's pregnancy exposes his sin. King David seeks to cover his tracks by bringing her husband, Uriah, back home from the front lines with hopes that he will have sexual relations with his wife, which would cause her pregnancy to be accepted without question. His plan is foiled when Uriah refuses the comforts of home, even after repeated attempts. So David abusively puts him in danger on the front lines with hopes that his life would be taken. Uriah dies. King David's plan works. His lust is kept secret. However, the Lord knows, so he sends the prophet Nathan to confront him. As a result of this confrontation, King David responds with a repentant heart (2 Samuel 11:25, 27; 12:1-13), which is captured fully in two psalms, Psalm 51 and 32.

Even though King David has a repentant heart and avoids the Law's prescribed penalty of death for both adultery and murder, he must still live with the consequences of his actions. He, too, experiences a fall. The latter part of the books of Samuel recounts the unfolding of these consequences. King David continues to live as a godly man, yet he lives with the reminders of his sin all around him. The consequences are felt most severely in his family.

King Solomon

King Solomon's rise is immediate. He is a royal figure almost from the beginning. King David has extended the kingdom, and the nation is experiencing much blessing from the Lord. Life is good in the Promised Land. For the most part, the details of his rise involve the revelation of his riches to the Queen of Sheba, which shows the unprecedented wealth of the king, and building both the palace and the Temple, further evidences of the many blessings the Lord pours out. As king, Solomon is revealed as perhaps the most powerful man in the world.

His turning point for King Solomon is, in one sense, subtle, as depicted in the previous chapter. But, in another sense, it is blatant, as found in 1 Kings 11. Verse 4 explains that this tragic turn of events occurs "when he is old." King Solomon turns away from the Lord. He sets up shrines for his wives, so that their gods can be worshipped and given honor, honor that belonged only to the Lord. The Lord is not happy about this turn of events for two reasons. First, the instructions for the king in Deuteronomy 17 clearly forbade the worship of other gods. They were to be wholly devoted to the Lord and lead the nation in the proper worship of the Lord. Second, the Lord had appeared to King Solomon twice, personally, to warn him of the consequences of turning his heart away. Solomon stubbornly walked away from the Lord and the life that is found in him, and him alone.

Solomon's fall is powerful and abrupt. Basically, the story of his life ends at this point. There is no opportunity given for confrontation or response. The story continues with some detailing of the tragic unfolding of events in the days following his rapid decline, but overall King Solomon's death is quickly announced. It is over. The kingdom is divided, and the nation never recovers from this moment, apart from periodic revivals. His fall affects each of the kings that follow. In other words, his fall is not just personal; it is national. The Lord is going to fulfill his purposes, but it is clear that it will not happen through the leadership of an earthly king. Solomon's fall is representative of every earthly king's fall. There will be no recovery. The prophets begin to reveal what will happen, slowly, but surely. A promised one is coming, the Messiah. The focus of THE STORY turns now to the rise of the king, the one who will come and set all things right. Any revivals that happen during the reigns of the kings that follow are simply foreshadows of a greater work that God is going to do in the future.

We must grasp this concept. God's kingdom on this earth will not be fulfilled through earthly leadership. Our goal is not to usher in the kingdom. Our goal is not a Christian government. Our goal is to live as kingdom people awaiting the coming King. Taking over an earthly government will not bring God's kingdom on earth. We await the arrival of God's kingdom, which will come to us only through the arrival of his Son, Jesus.

As we have noted, each king has a rise, a turning point, and a fall. However, of the three kings, King David is set forth as the model king. Every good king of any prominence who follows him is distinguished as a king "like David." What is different about King David, when for all practical purposes he seems to have botched his life just like Saul and Solomon? Is there some clue in his life that offers a lesson for us to learn? This leads to the second theological point of these three kings.

Repentance

The second theological point emphasized by the story of these three kings is a proper response to the exposure of sin in our lives. King David is sandwiched between Kings Saul and Solomon, and his life presents a contrast. All three of them sin defiantly, but the difference is in their response when confronted. A closer examination reveals an important theological point for us: God's concern is not whether we sin or not because this is a theological given. We are sinners even though God has made us new creatures in Christ. God's concern is how we respond to our sin when it is exposed and brought to the light.

When King Saul's sin is exposed the story presents

him as one who wanted to, and even tried to, obey, but in the end his fears and selfish desires dominated his decisions and actions. Remember, when he was confronted he shifted the blame (1 Samuel 15:21), rationalized his actions (1 Samuel 13:11-12; 15:15, 24), and minimized his disobedience (1 Samuel 15:25). Each of these responses shows disrespect for the word of the Lord and his glory.

King Solomon's sin is exposed without much opportunity for response. The point made as his idolatry is confronted is that the Lord had forewarned him of this sin twice. His sin is confronted, judgment is given, and Solomon is not heard from again. The assumption is that he is so steeped in his sin that there is no return. His sin is blatant, and he is past the point of no return. His lack of repentance demonstrates the hardness and direction of his heart.

King David is a great contrast. Initially, before he is confronted, he seeks to manipulate the situation to cover his sin. This occurs in two stages. First, he attempts to bring Uriah home from the front lines to give him a report of the battle. This, however, is a ploy intended to encourage him to have sexual relations with his wife, which would make it appear that this was the cause of Bathsheba's pregnancy. People would believe that her pregnancy was the result of the day when Uriah came home to give his report. Uriah foils the plan when he refuses to have sexual relations with his wife while his fellow warriors were in the midst of battle. So Uriah goes back to the front lines, and King David still has a problem. Second, David has Joab, the military commander, put Uriah in danger by advancing too close to the wall of the enemy city. Again, this is simply a ploy on David's part. His plan is to put Uriah in harm's way so he will die. When he dies, David will bring Bathsheba into his house, and her pregnancy will then be the result of their new relationship. As a result, his adultery would not be exposed. Both of these stages are a manipulative abuse of power to cover his adultery, and he can do this because he is king and has the power.

After David covers up his "mess," he is confronted by Nathan, the prophet. Nathan masterfully tells a story of injustice, and then indicts David with the words, "You are the man." Obviously, King David has the power to end Nathan's life. He does not, and unlike Saul, he also does not shift blame, rationalize his actions, or minimize his disobedience. Instead, we see the humility of David's heart. He owns his sin, is repentant, and turns his heart back to the Lord, seeking his mercy (Psalm 32 and 51). This is why his life is held up as one to be emulated. Because our sin is a given, the Lord seeks for us to be humble and turn back to him when our sin is exposed. David does this.

The text seeks to make this plain for us. In 2 Samuel 11:25, King David tells Joab, "Do not let this thing be evil in your eyes." However, the Lord has a different perspective than King David as found in verse 27, "but this thing was evil in the eyes of the Lord." Therein lies the problem. When we see our actions differently than the Lord does, we are on dangerous ground. David basically says, "Don't let this bother you...it's no big deal." But it is a big deal for the Lord. It bothers him. Until we see as the Lord sees, our hearts will not know repentance.

Repentance becomes obvious in Psalm 51, a psalm that is supposedly written when King David is wrestling with his conscience at this time. In verse four he writes, "I have done what is evil in your eyes." His perspective of the situation now matches the Lord's. As a result, he repents, and his heart turns back to the Lord. Standing in contrast to Saul and Solomon, King David demonstrates a proper response to the exposure of his sin. He humbly acknowledges the Lord's supremacy and sees life through the Lord's word. This enables him to turn from his evil ways and follow the Lord, his sovereign God. That is how we are to handle our sin too.

We must see this emphasis when we read these books, and we should celebrate it. Blessed be the name of the Lord, who is merciful to us as we turn our hearts to him in our sin. His loving-kindness does indeed live forever.

Making It Real

1)   Your life is probably full of the same pattern as these kings'. You have experienced rises, turning points, and falls. For some the pattern is intense, for others it is subtle. Nonetheless, it is the experience of everyone who seeks to faithfully follow the Lord. What leads to turning points in your life? Are there habits that inhibit them? Are there habits that encourage them? Create a list of habits or practices (some might say spiritual disciplines) that help keep your heart oriented toward the Lord and inhibit turning away from the Lord.

2)   Does the Lord's loving-kindness run out? Does it fail? Has the Lord ever turned you away when your heart turned back to him after a period of rebellion? Take some time to thank the Lord.

3)   Or maybe you have been in a time of rebellion and your hardened heart refuses to turn back to the Lord. Consider once again his loving-kindness. It is available to you. He longs for you to return to him so that he can pour out his blessings on you. If you need to return, let this be the time for you to repent and receive the Lord's mercy.

4)   Perhaps your heart is breaking because a friend of family member is running from the Lord. Pray that the Lord would poured out his mercy. Pray that your loved one's heart will soften and receive the Lord's tender mercies. Pray that they would repent.

CHAPTER NINETEEN:
1 AND 2 KINGS

As we come to the books of Kings, we are now well versed in the kingdom. We have already had two kings, Saul and David. Their lives present a contrast, which will be a model for all we read in the books of Kings. The principle of the Davidic Covenant will be clear. When a king walks in obedience to the Mosaic Covenant, as David did, there will be blessings galore. However, when a king walks in disobedience, as Saul did, there will be consequences for the nation. The books of Kings pick up THE STORY at this point, focusing on King Solomon in order to emphasize the building of the Temple at the beginning. Then, for the remainder of the book, the focus turns to a quick summary of the kings that followed detailing their obedience or disobedience. A few extended and significant stories are also recorded.

The title of the book in Hebrew means "kings." It is as simple as that. The title, therefore, captures the emphasis of the books. These books are about kings. As I mentioned in the chapter on the books of Samuel, the Greek translation, the Septuagint, lists the books of Kings as 3 and 4 Kings, with the books of Samuel being 1 and 2 Kings. Uniting the books into a unit of four books underscores their common focus.

The book does not provide a clear identification of authorship. The Talmud ascribes it to Jeremiah. Many scholars have offered insights that support this supposition, but that is not important for our purposes. At some point, an author compiled this history to give a broad overview of the nation during this period. As we will see, there is a theological point to the writing of this history.

Major Divisions

The books begin at the conclusion of the story of King David, and it is obvious that they continue THE STORY already written in the books of Samuel. Again, this is one of the many reasons for us to view the four books as a unit. However, for our purposes here, let's set forth an outline of the two books of Kings:

I.   1 Kings 1-11, "The United Kingdom."

During this time, Solomon is ruling over the nation. The twelve tribes are united, and the blessing of the Lord is obvious to see as the people prosper and the borders of the nation are expanded.

II.   1 Kings 12 – 2 Kings 18, "The Divided Kingdom"

During this time, the kingdom is divided as a consequence of Solomon's sin. The 10 tribes in the north comprise the northern kingdom of Israel. The two tribes in the south comprise the southern kingdom of Judah. In these chapters we read the stories of many kings who ruled in either the northern or the southern kingdoms. The stories are told somewhat sequentially, but there is much jumping around from northern kingdom to southern kingdom, making the narrative difficult to read. At the end of this section, the northern kingdom is removed from the land because of her continued rebellion, leaving only the southern kingdom of Judah.

III.   2 Kings 18-25, "The Southern Kingdom's Final Years"

During this time, only the southern kingdom of Judah remains in the land. In these chapters we read of many kings who ruled the kingdom. This period ends with the overthrow of the southern kingdom, which followed the northern kingdom's path of rebellion. As a result, at the end of the books of Kings, no kingdom remains.

The books end on a very sad note. Remember, however, that the Lord is making a way so the Davidic Covenant will not be nullified by Israel's (or Judah's) disobedience. The Lord will continue to advance his plans and accomplish his purposes to the glory of his great name.

Main Message

The main message of the books is the glory and division of Israel. Under Solomon, the reign is glorious as blessing is poured out on the nation. After his sin and the division of the kingdom, there is much struggle as the people continue to rebel against their covenant with the Lord.

The books focus on the people primarily responsible for keeping the covenant, the kings and the prophets. Deuteronomy 17:14-20 provides the stipulations for a king, and one of these is that he is to write out a copy of the law and not depart from it to the left or the right. He is to be the one who points the nation toward obedience by the way he lives and leads the nation. The prophets are the primary means the Lord uses to keep obedient kings focused on the right path and call rebellious kings back to obedience. Their ministry is rarely tangential as they confront the kings on several occasions. Generally, they end up hated by the king which leads to their death, or they profound influence the direction of the kingdom as the king repents and turns the kingdom back to the Lord. Kings had the power to affect the direction of the kingdom. The choices they made rippled throughout the land. An easy way to remember this principle is: as the king goes, so go the people. And the prophet had the potential to affect the king's direction. Once again, the principle of the Davidic Covenant is very important:

If a king was obedient to the Mosaic Law by worshipping the Lord exclusively, desiring to live out the law and love one's neighbor in a way that honored the Lord, and perpetuating the covenant to each generation, then the nation would be blessed and would know peace and rest from their enemies, prosperity in their work, and the expansion of their borders. However, if a king was disobedient to the Mosaic Law by worshipping other gods, not living out the law in a manner that honored one's neighbor, and disregarding the perpetuation of the covenant to future generations, then the nation would be judged and would know defeat and oppression from their enemies, failure and difficulty in their work, and ultimately exile into foreign lands.

As long as a king lived obediently to the Mosaic Covenant and led the people toward the Lord, Israel was the best place in the world to live as they enjoyed blessings from the hand of the Lord.

The books Kings cover the time period from the end of King David's reign (around 970 BC) to the Babylonian conquest of Jerusalem (around 586 BC) by focusing on selective events and covering the kingdom's highest and lowest points. During Solomon's reign the nation experienced unprecedented blessing. Similar blessings came during the reign of other kings, however, under the watch of many other kings the nation experienced the tragedy of disobedience, including exile from the land.

KING SOLOMON'S REIGN

The first part of the book occurs when the kingdom is united and focuses on the reign of King Solomon. The book begins with the events surrounding King David's death and the subsequent battle for the throne. David's first and third born sons are dead (2 Samuel 13-18). His second born son is not mentioned after 2 Samuel 3, so he is presumed dead. The fourth born son (2 Samuel 3:2-5), Adonijah, begins the process of taking what he thinks will be rightfully his. But Nathan the prophet steps in and advises Bathsheba according to the Lord's word to David in 1 Chronicles 22:8-10,

> But the word of the LORD came to me, saying, "You have shed much blood and have waged great wars. You shall not build a house to my name, because you

have shed so much blood before me on the earth. Behold, a son shall be born to you who shall be a man of rest. I will give him rest from all his surrounding enemies. For his name shall be Solomon, and I will give peace and quiet to Israel in his days. He shall build a house for my name. He shall be my son, and I will be his father, and I will establish his royal throne in Israel forever."

In this passage, Solomon is clearly identified as the one who is to take the throne.

Overall, Solomon's reign is marked by blessing, but there are initial signs of trouble, which show that this blessing is not necessarily contingent on his absolute obedience. In 1 Kings 3:1-3, we are quickly confronted with his marriage alliance with Pharaoh, king of Egypt. Marriage alliances always point toward a strengthening of one's position politically, rather than fully trusting in the Lord. So, ultimately, it constitutes a lack of trust. We also see other minor issues, which seem to indicate that all is not well, such as in the building of the Temple the use of "I have built" (cf. 1 Kings 8:13, 14, 27, 43, 44, 48). He seems focused on his accomplishments rather than on the Lord's work through him. Additionally, the contrast of his palace with the Temple stands out as we examine his life. 1 Kings 6:38 says that it took seven years to build the Temple, but 1

Kings 7:1 notes that it took thirteen years to build his own house. This is quite a contrast between the "house of the Lord" and the king's personal residence.

However, the strongest indictment of Solomon is found in 1 Kings 10:14-11:3. We must read this passage with Deuteronomy 17:14-20, which identifies the requirements of a king, as a backdrop. By comparing these two passages, we find that King Solomon was making some horrible decisions. Consider this chart:

Deuteronomy 17:14-20	1 Kings 10:14-11:3
A man of the Lord's choosing	1 Chronicles 22:8-10 gives a clear word from the Lord that he chose Solomon to be king
An Israelite	From Bethlehem, of the tribe of Judah, 1 Samuel 16
Must not multiply horses, especially from Egypt	Multiplied horses, even from Egypt, 1 Kings 10:26-29
Must not multiply wives	Multiplied wives, 1 Kings 11:1-3, even from the nations the Lord commanded the people to not marry (Deuteronomy 7:1-7)
Must not multiply gold or silver	Multiplied much gold and silver, 1 Kings 10:14-24

Must write out a copy of the Law so that he can lead the people in the ways of the Lord	No record of this ever happening for King Solomon, but we do know that he excelled in wisdom, which comes from the Lord (and his word)

So, the abrupt and tragic conclusion to Solomon's reign in 1 Kings 11:4-43 is actually not so abrupt. He had been sowing these seeds throughout his life, culminating in building shrines to foreign gods to satisfy his wives and the people (1Kings 11:4-8). As a result, this wise man's life ends on a tragic note.

The major consequence of King Solomon's poor decisions is the division of the kingdom (1 Kings 12:16-24). Although passages like 2 Samuel 20:10 and 1 Kings 12:16 hint at struggles between north and south before there was actually a Northern and Southern Kingdom, this division is not official until this time in Israel's history. The remaining chapters in the books of Kings focus on brief summaries of the kings who reigned in both kingdoms. The central issue is always whether or not they follow the Law.

THE NORTHERN KINGDOM

The Northern Kingdom lasts a little over 200 years

and is ruled by 19 kings (or 20, if Tibni is included; 1 Kings 16:21). This is an unstable period because the kings are very ungodly. Since they fail to follow the Lord, there is much political unrest with an average reign of only 10 years. Rather than passing the throne from father to son, we find nine different ruling families. Seven kings are assassinated. One king commits suicide. One is stricken by God. One is exiled to Assyria. All the kings of the Northern Kingdom were evil. They perpetuated the worship of the golden calf, which was introduced by Jereboam after a sojourn in Egypt (1 Kings 12:25-33). You might note the connection between the golden calf worship of Exodus 32 and the people's departure from Egypt on that occasion as well. The Lord who gave Israel the Promised Land was removed from his rightful place as king and rejected by his people.

As a result of the kingdom's continuous evil, the Lord eventually takes them into exile in Assyria. Their evil was an abomination to the Lord, and ultimately they lived like the people who were originally driven from the land. 2 Kings 17:7-23 summarizes why the Lord sent the people into exile. The land was full of idolatrous worship to the point that worshipping the gods of the land had risen above worshipping the Lord. They looked to, trusted in, and worshipped gods of wood and stone. The Lord was being denigrated. In Leviticus 18:24-30, the Lord had warned the people of the consequences of such rebellion:

> Do not make yourselves unclean by any of these things, for by all these the nations I am driving out before you have become unclean, and the land became unclean, so that I punished its iniquity, and the land vomited out its inhabitants. But you shall keep my statutes and my rules and do none of these abominations, either the native or the stranger who sojourns among you (for the people of the land, who were before you, did all of these abominations, so that the land became unclean), lest the land vomit you out when you make it unclean, as it vomited out the nation that was before you. For everyone who does any of these abominations, the persons who do them shall be cut off from among their people. So keep my charge never to practice any of these abominable customs that were practiced before you, and never to make yourselves unclean by them: I am the LORD your God.

But the people did not heed this warning and the Northern Kingdom never recovers.

THE SOUTHERN KINGDOM

The Southern Kingdom is not much better, but there

are a few positive moments. This kingdom lasts about 350 years and is ruled by 19 kings and one queen. Apart from Queen Athaliah, there is one ruling family, the lineage of King David. There is more stability as the average reign of each king is 17 years, but there is still a lot of political instability as five kings are assassinated, three are exiled to foreign lands, and two are stricken by God. All the kings but eight are evil. These eight good kings lead the people in returning to the Lord. Under their leadership, we get a glimpse of what the Lord intended for his people as he blesses the nation, which bows to him and lives for his glory.

King David's continued lineage underscores a significant theological point in the Old Testament: God is making a way, advancing his plans, and he will accomplish his purposes. In the midst of much political turmoil in both the Northern and Southern Kingdoms, the Lord raises up godly kings who return the people to covenant faithfulness. The Lord also continues the Messianic line by preserving David's family. Note the strong contrast of nine different ruling families in the Northern Kingdom and the maintenance of the one ruling family in the Southern. This ensures the fulfillment of the Davidic Covenant's promises and the Lord's plans to redeem his people.

The focus in the closing chapters of 2 Kings is on the

attempts at reform by godly kings whom the Lord raised up. It is not enough to reverse the eventual exile of this kingdom as well, but it is enough to keep the Lord's plans for his people moving forward. In the end, the Southern Kingdom receives the same fate as the Northern. They go into exile at the hands of the new world power, the Babylonians. However, they remain distinct as a people, and they one day return to the land to continue the Lord's plans.

Context in THE STORY

The books of Kings pick up THE STORY from the end of the books of Samuel. In fact, these four books (Samuel and Kings) provide the continuous narrative of the kingdom. There were three major kings: Saul, David, and Solomon, and numerous kings in the divided kingdom. The narrative focus is on contrasting Saul, a picture of what happens when a king is not faithful to the covenant, and David, a picture of what happens when a king is faithful to the covenant. This is the foundation for understanding the brief stories of the many kings of the divided kingdom. King Solomon's story explains why the kingdom was divided. Both kingdoms end up in a bad place as both are exiled. The Northern Kingdom basically disappears from THE STORY, but the Southern Kingdom only disappears temporarily, for a period of 70 years. To understand more of what the nation experienced during this period, it is important to read books like Daniel or Jeremiah. However, THE STORY picks up again in the books of Ezra and Nehemiah, which tell the story of the people's return to the land. They will not become a kingdom, but they will seek to act like the people of the Lord once more.

Looking Forward to Jesus

The books of Kings repeatedly demonstrate the failures of earthly kings. Periodically, we find a king "like David" who lives in a manner that honors the Lord, but, overall, all the kings in the northern kingdom of Israel are evil and all but eight of the kings in the southern kingdom of Judah are evil. However, even the good kings are fallible and struggle with sin. The people's hope cannot rest in an earthly king, nor can it rest in an earthly kingdom. The kings live faithfully, but they are still sinful and need a Savior. These good kings point to and remind the people of the future king who will fulfill 2 Samuel 7, the one who will sit on the forever throne, ruling with justice and righteousness. This king will rule "to the ends of the earth" and will be "our peace" (Micah 5:1-5a). As the people struggled, their hearts began to long for the coming king. This longing grows through the prophetic books. Anticipation begins. A king is coming. Hope is revived.

CHAPTER TWENTY:
THE THEOLOGY OF 1 AND 2 KINGS

Let us begin with some background material. From the very beginning the Lord had warned Israel of the dangers of idolatry and the influence the gods of the nations could have on them. As they entered into a covenant relationship with the Lord at Mt. Sinai and were given the 10 commandments, the Lord says in Exodus 20:2-6,

I am the LORD your God, who brought you out of the land of Egypt, out of the house of slavery. You shall have no other gods before me. You shall not make for yourself a carved image, or any likeness of anything that is in heaven above, or that is in the earth beneath, or that is in the water under the earth. You shall not bow down to them or serve them, for I, the LORD your God, am a jealous God, visiting the iniquity of the fathers on the children to the third and the fourth generation of those who hate me, but showing steadfast love to thousands of those who love me and keep my commandments.

This commandment is central to what it meant for the nation to belong to the Lord. Similar commands are also provided in Exodus 23:20-33 and 34:6-17. In Exodus 23:13, the Lord says, "Pay attention to all that I have said to you, and make no mention of the names of other gods, nor let it be heard on your lips." This underscores the seriousness of even beginning to move away from the Lord. The Lord is saying, "Do not even open the door for such talk."

Two reasons are provided for this prohibition. First, there is no one like the Lord. His name, from Yahweh in Hebrew, is the Lord, which means: I am the one who is with you and will be for you. That is powerful! Second, the Lord is a jealous God (Exodus 20:5; 34:14; see also Deuteronomy 6:15; 4:24; 5:9; Joshua 24:19; and Nahum 1:2). Relationship with the Lord is to be an exclusive one, which means that worshipping another god is committing adultery. So, Israel was called to covenant fidelity and faithfulness to one God.

Deuteronomy 7:1-7 is key to understanding this principle (see also 12:1-5; 16:21; Leviticus 20:2-5), with verses 2-6 providing the rationale when read backwards. The people are holy, devoted to the Lord, and they are to remain so; and they are not to give their hearts to another god but are to remain holy, devoted to the Lord. How does this happen? By destroying the people in the land and their gods.

Israel did not heed these warnings, so she quickly encounters the consequences. Although the book of Joshua seemingly summarizes the obedience of the people, the book of Judges reveals some deeper issues, which create havoc for the nation. Judges 2:12-13 reads, "And they abandoned the LORD, the God of their fathers, who had brought them out of the land of Egypt. They went after other gods, from among the gods of the peoples who were around them, and bowed down to them. And they provoked the LORD to anger. They abandoned the LORD and served the Baals and the Ashtaroth." They did not heed the warnings of Deuteronomy 7. The people do not remain holy, devoted to the Lord. Judges 3:3-7 explains further,

These are the nations: the five lords of the Philistines and all the Canaanites and the Sidonians and the Hivites who lived on Mount Lebanon, from Mount

Baal-hermon as far as Lebo-hamath. They were for the testing of Israel, to know whether Israel would obey the commandments of the LORD, which he commanded their fathers by the hand of Moses. So the people of Israel lived among the Canaanites, the Hittites, the Amorites, the Perizzites, the Hivites, and the Jebusites. And their daughters they took to themselves for wives, and their own daughters they gave to their sons, and they served their gods. And the people of Israel did what was evil in the sight of the LORD. They forgot the LORD their God and served the Baals and the Asheroth.

This is the undoing of Deuteronomy 7. The people did the opposite of what the Lord commanded them, and the Lord's word on what would happen if they did comes true. Israel is in a bad place, and ultimately this situation remains for her.

In one sense, Israel is never able to overcome the consequences as she remains in struggle throughout her history apart from some brief periods of revival. Throughout the period of the kingdom we see evidence of idolatry (see 1 Kings 11:4-8, 31-33; 16:30-33). Although there are some periods when the idolatrous practices are destroyed (see 1 Kings 18:16-36; 2 Kings 18:3-6; 23:4-15), this situation dominates their history. This destructive influence is a constant weakness of the people, and they miss out on the Lord's blessings. They are continuously gripped by idolatry. As you read this part of Israel's history, there are many gods you will encounter.

The issue for Israel was always the power believed to be behind the idol. They had struggles in life, and they thought these gods would succeed for them in ways the Lord could not or in ways that the Lord had "failed."

When was the last time you bowed to an idol? For most of you, this is an odd question. I used to get my hair cut by a Vietnamese woman. As I entered her shop, there was a statute of Buddha with a bowl for gifts. I can honestly say that I never had a struggle with bowing down and worshipping that idol of offering a gift in hopes of gaining an advantage from that god's powers. I must confess that I did contemplate grabbing one of the apples in the bowl from time to time for myself. Joking aside, in western culture, most of us probably do not struggle with bowing to idols and worshipping them. So is there any meaning for us in Israel's struggle? Yes, and we must understand that though we may not struggle with bowing to idols, our hearts can turn away from the Lord to worship other "gods" just like Israel.

To better understand this, we must understand the essence of idolatry. Isaiah 44 provides insight into the battle we all face, whether we bow to idols or not, beginning with the Garden of Eden. Isaiah 44:6-8 sets forth the greatness of the Lord. In verses nine and following, the prophet reveals the folly of idols. A block of wood used for normal human functions like building a fire for warmth and baking bread is also fashioned into a shape and worshipped. This is ludicrous, but it is the reality of idolatry. This should remind us of Romans 1, where Paul observes humanity's tendency to worship the creature rather than the Creator. Ludicrous! However, it is not simply an idol that is the problem; rather it is the heart behind it. Verse 17 states, "And the rest of it he makes into a god, his idol, and falls down to it and worships it. He prays to it and says, 'Deliver me, for you are my god!'" These words capture the essence of idolatry: "Deliver me, for you are my god." Whatever or whoever we look to for deliverance becomes our god. Here is the principle:

> We will worship whatever brings us the life that we want in the world now. If it "works," we try to justify it, rationalize it, make it fit into our relationship with God, and even exalt it above God, because it makes our world "better."

Just like Adam and Eve in the garden, we worship the creature rather than the Creator. We look to a piece of fruit to bring us something we think God might be withholding from us. Just like Israel, we worship the creature rather than the Creator. We look to the powers that be—wealth, position, power, relationships, pornography, various addictions—to bring us something we think God might be withholding from us. Ludicrous!

Jeremiah 44 makes this even clearer. The nation has been warned of their rebellion and idolatry. In verses 15-19, they affirm their position, saying,

Then all the men who knew that their wives had made offerings to other gods, and all the women who stood by, a great assembly, all the people who lived in Pathros in the land of Egypt, answered Jeremiah: "As for the word that you have spoken to us in the name of the LORD, we will not listen to you. But we will do everything that we have vowed, make offerings to the queen of heaven and pour out drink offerings to her, as we did, both we and our fathers, our kings and our officials, in the cities of Judah and in the streets of Jerusalem. For then we had plenty of food, and prospered, and saw no disaster. But since we left off making offerings to the queen of heaven and pouring out drink offerings to her, we have lacked everything and have been consumed by the sword and by famine."

Essentially the people are saying that God was not working for them, but they had found something else that was. That is the tendency of humanity. Whatever seems to bring us life receives our worship. When we fail to see the beauty of the Lord in all his glory, we often move toward a lesser "god" to have our needs met. In effect we will cry out, "Deliver me for you are my god!" Ludicrous, yet we do it.

That was the problem, yet Israel failed to see it. She was so steeped in her culture that she struggled to see how she was going astray. The worldview of the day had so permeated her mind and heart that she failed to see the dilemma it created for those who sought to honor the Lord above all. If this is true for Israel, it can be true for us as well. Has our present culture and the worldview that predominates influenced your own mind and heart to the point that you justify the "gods" you worship? Ludicrous, yet we do it. May the Lord reveal our "gods" to us and grant us the mercy to turn away from that which does not give life and turn to the one who does.

Making It Real

1)   Be honest and make a list of the "gods" of your culture. What/who do people worship? What do people believe these "gods" will do for those who honor them.

2)   In your own heart and in discussion with others

honestly reflect on what or who you might trust in when difficulties arise? Who/what do you look to for deliverance? What "works" for you? The difficulty in determining these "gods" is that, like Israel, we seek to justify and rationalize them. Pray and ask the Lord to help you see your "gods."

3) Understand that we do not simply repent of "gods" and they are gone. This is a battle that will continue until the Lord returns. Pray for the church, your close friends, and your own heart that the Lord would help you maintain purity and forsake the "gods" of this world.

CHAPTER TWENTY-ONE:
THE POETIC BOOKS

The poetic books bring us into the framework of everyday living for the nation of Israel. They provide an expression of faith from individual Israelites or the nation as a whole and reflect on how to live in a covenantal relationship with the Lord. Life presents many challenges, and the poetic books record the reactions, reflections, and emotions of one who is trying to remain faithful to the Mosaic Covenant in the midst of it all. Although much of what is recorded in these books is connected to THE STORY, the historical context is not as important since these books deal with timeless issues confronting all of humanity.

People like to read the poetic books because they are filled with emotion. As people live, they feel, and as most of us know, feelings are not always rational. The poetic books do not seek a logical development; rather they are often raw expressions of struggle in the midst of a life that often makes no sense. Because of this, people identify with the complaints, unexpected joys, and troublesome situations of the poets and wise men. A psalm such as Psalm 23 is timeless, providing comfort for all generations.

Main Message

The main message of the poetic books deals with the complexity of living every day with the goal of praising the Lord in the midst of life. These issues are investigated by a variety of godly men who the Lord used to provide insight into daily living. For our purposes, each book will be given a brief synopsis in order to summarize its contents.

JOB

Job is the first of the poetic books. The title is simply the main character's name, although he could have been the author as well. The events recorded in the book probably occurred during the time of the Patriarchs (Abraham, Isaac, Jacob, and Joseph). This is supported by details like: Job lived 140 years after his losses, which corresponds with the longer lives common during this period (42:16); Job's wealth was measured in terms of livestock which is also similar to this period (1:3); Job's function as priest in his home is another characteristic of this period (1:5); and the absence of Israel and the Mosaic Law suggests an earlier date. The date of writing could have been shortly after the events took place or at a later time in history. The detailed speeches seem to support an earlier date.

There are some who believe that Job was not an actual person and the events of the book did not really occur. This is based on the book's unique beginning and ending. Job's fortune and family at the beginning of the book is lost, but at the end his family is restored to exactly the same proportions (7 sons and 3 daughters) and his fortune is exactly doubled. Because this is rather remarkable, the book is understood to be a parable. However, throughout the Bible, Job is understood to be a real person (see passages like Ezekiel 14:14). The Lord is at work in this world and in people's lives to accomplish his purposes, and Job presents a unique picture of the ways he works.

Job is a book about suffering. It is technically called a theodicy, which is defined as a vindication of God in the face of suffering and evil. The story helps us wrestle with the age old question of why the righteous suffer. Job's counselors conclude that righteous people do not suffer, which is basically good Old Testament theology. Throughout the Old Testament it is clear that obedience brings blessing and disobedience brings discipline. It is modeled in the Garden, supported in the destruction of the world by the flood and of Sodom and Gomorrah by fire, and a central component of the Mosaic Covenant (see Leviticus 26 or Deuteronomy 28). Job's counselors do not know how to approach Job's situation from any other angle. He is experiencing obvious discipline, therefore, he needs to turn from his sin. However, this book shows that the Lord works above and beyond what he communicates to us. He knows more and does what is best, whether righteous people experience his blessings or not. He is more concerned about the growth of righteous people and their knowledge of him than he is about their enjoyment of his blessings.

Job learns that the Lord is worthy of love and worship even when his life hits bottom. In the end, Job proves Satan wrong. Not only does he not curse the Lord when Satan wreaks havoc on his life, his love for and worship of the Lord deepens and becomes more real. Job was stripped of everything, but his trust in the Lord became stronger.

PSALMS

Psalms is probably one of the most popular books in the Bible. Even if someone does not believe the Bible, they may quote verses from the Psalms at funerals or weddings.

The English title, Psalms, is taken from the Greek translation of the Old Testament. It is translated as "songs" or "poems sung with musical accompaniment." In the Hebrew, the title is translated as "praise." This Hebrew title provides a good summary of the contents. Psalms is actually comprised of five separate books (1-41, 42-72, 73-89, 90-106, and 107-150). Tradition concludes that the five books were to correspond with the five books of the Pentateuch, and each ends with a doxology of praise. Psalms 145-150 provide a doxology at the end of the collection. This demonstrates why the book is entitled "Praise" in the Hebrew Bible.

Authorship varies from psalm to psalm. King David is the primary author, having written most of the psalms recorded for us. Other authors include Asaph, the Korahites, King Solomon, Ethan, and even Moses. There are also a number of anonymously written psalms. With King David being the primary author, the psalms basically fit into the story of the kingdom, especially during David's reign. Most of the other psalms are authored by groups or individuals, who also lived during this period.

There are psalms of lament, praise, repentance, and wisdom, not to mention messianic psalms, just to name a few. In other words, psalms were penned out of a variety of situations. In addition, some concern individuals and are very personal, while others have a corporate focus and are more generic. Some psalms have a prescript that connect the psalm to a specific historical event and provide a deeper understanding of the events surrounding the writing.

The book of Psalms is about worship. Even when a psalmist is working through difficulty, the psalm generally finds its way to a proper focus on God's sovereignty or majesty. As such, we learn that even in the most difficult circumstances, God can be found, embraced, trusted, and worshipped. They help us find hope, comfort, and words with which to worship. They help us express our own emotions, which may have been previously suppressed. Because of this we can grow through experiences with the psalmist's help. These psalms transcend time and minister to many who read them today.

PROVERBS

This book is just what the title says, a book of proverbial statements, which provide instruction about life. Proverbs are short, often catchy, sayings, which communicate truths in the fewest words possible. The Hebrew word means "comparison," as many proverbs provide a comparison or antithesis. So this book seeks to provide moral and spiritual instruction for those who want to live wisely. With this as its goal, it is no wonder that so many look to this book for practical advice. In fact, because the book has 31 chapters, it can be read through every month simply by reading a chapter per day.

Most of this book is attributed to King Solomon, so the historical context is that of the kingdom, specifically during his reign. Other authors are mentioned including: "the wise," Agur, King Lemuel, and a committee who selected certain proverbs for a collection. It is not as important to know the historical context when reading this book, but it is interesting to note when they were penned and by whom. In fact, as we look at King Solomon's life, we see that, at the end, he was not able to heed his own proverbial advice.

The book is more than a series of short, wise statements to be applied to everyday life. Chapters 1-9 are more doctrinal, setting forth a worldview necessary for living in the fear of the Lord. This worldview understands, first, that the Lord has ordained a particular structure or flow of living in this world. He is the Creator, and he has designed this world in such a way that his creatures can experience blessing if they live in a certain way. Second, this worldview addresses the desires of created beings. These desires are good and God-given, but they must be aligned with the Lord's design. The popular passage found in 3:5-12 captures this worldview:

Trust in the LORD with all your heart, and do not lean on your own understanding.

In all your ways acknowledge him, and he will make straight your paths.

Be not wise in your own eyes; fear the LORD, and turn away from evil.

It will be healing to your flesh and refreshment to your bones.

Honor the LORD with your wealth and with the first fruits of all your produce;

then your barns will be filled with plenty, and your vats will be bursting with wine.

My son, do not despise the LORD's discipline or be weary of his reproof,

for the LORD reproves him whom he loves, as a father the son in whom he delights.

It is only by aligning ourselves with the Lord and fearing him that the desires of our hearts will be fulfilled.

In these early chapters, there are 4 main characters: son, father, wisdom, and the strange woman. The father seeks to inform the son of the choices represented by wisdom and the strange woman. The overall point is that the strange woman will lead to death and misalignment with God's design, but wisdom will lead to life and proper alignment with God's design. The choice is set before the reader, and it is obvious which is best.

After the worldview has been set forth, chapters 10-31 apply it. This is the part that contains the short, wise statements. They offer advice for all who read, advice that must be heeded if we want to experience the blessings of living according to God's design. Note, however, that these proverbs are not promises. They are observations of a wise person who has looked broadly at a number of situations and offered advice on the best choice in light of what it means to live in proper alignment with God's design. The goal is to help people live wisely, and through the years this book has been a treasure to those who have read it.

ECCLESIATES

Ecclesiastes is a popular book for debate, but its basic theme is the futility of living outside of God's purposes. If life is only lived "under the sun," then futility will be the experience. The title of this book comes from the Greek translation, and it means "assembly." The Hebrew title means "preacher" or "one who speaks at an assembly." In other words, this book is penned to a group of people by someone with an important message to communicate.

It has generally been accepted that King Solomon is the author based on the following descriptions:

*son of David, king in Jerusalem (1:1)

*great wisdom, surpassing all before him (1:16)

*great wealth, more than any before him (2:7)

*easy opportunity for pleasure (2:3)

*massive building projects (2:4-6)

King Solomon fits each of these descriptors, and it would be difficult to find a rival to his successes. So, with King Solomon as the author, we have a historical context for this book as well. Reading the story of his life along with this book adds a depth of understanding.

The point of this book parallels the teaching of other wisdom literature. The fact that life is futile apart from God is developed throughout the book. King Solomon shows that putting confidence in earthly achievements and wisdom, apart from God, is futile. He continues to note that there is much in life that cannot be understood or controlled. Humanity is left to live by faith and trust God for the outcome. Further, like Job and unlike Proverbs, King Solomon points to the inconsistencies of living in a fallen world. Righteous people do not always "win the day." There are times when the unrighteous prevail. And, finally, the king makes it clear that we are not created to live on our own. Left to find our way in this world on our own, we will find emptiness and frustration. We are not designed to live that way. So is it all hopeless?

Does all end in futility? This book's answer is "No!" Meaning and significance can be found in fearing the Lord. To live "under the sun" we must properly fear the Lord. We must live with an awareness that the Lord is the Creator and Ruler over all. Contentment is found only in him and living for his purposes. The point is found in 12:13, "Fear God and keep his commandments; for this is the whole duty of man."

SONG OF SONGS

This book has been the source of much debate through the years. The basic issue has been how to understand it. Is it an allegory in which the contents have a deeper meaning typifying the relationship between God and his people? Much can be gleaned from this book and applied to this relationship, but this is not the purpose of the book. Is it both literal and allegorical with the contents relating specific historical events, yet still having a deeper meaning? So, in the end, the point is not a romantic one, but rather offers a picture of Christ's love for the church? Or should we read it literally as a secular love song, expressing human love in a very romantic tone? I believe this is the proper way to read the book. It is historical from the life of King Solomon. It is real. It is sexual. It is a love affair. It conveys truth about an important part of what it means to be human. It does not have to spiritualized, for our sexuality is spiritual in and of itself. There will naturally be many connections between human love and God's love for his people. Ephesians 5 reverses this and teaches that the love between a husband and wife is a picture of a deeper reality, that of Christ and his church. So it is not an error to avoid any analogous applications to God's love for his people. However, it is an error to avoid this important teaching about romantic love, which is at the core of intimate, opposite sex, relationships.

The title of the book has been given as "Song of Solomon," which is a compilation of the words in 1:1, "the song of songs, which is Solomon's." The preferred title, which is the same as the Hebrew title, is "Song of Songs," taken directly from 1:1. In the Hebrew this construction is a superlative and means, "the best of songs." Authorship is debated, but King Solomon is typically attributed authorship. His name is mentioned seven times (1:1, 5; 3:7, 9 11; 8:11-12). He is identified as the groom in the love story. 1:1 states that this best song is from Solomon (1 Kings 4:32 reminds us that Solomon wrote 1,005 songs). So the historical setting of this book is to be found in the life of King Solomon.

The book is written like a play with several scenes shifting the location and purpose. There are three main characters: the bride (Shulamite), the king (Solomon), and a chorus (daughters of Jerusalem). The book is a love story. It sets forth God's view of love and marriage through this description of physical love between a man and a woman.

Context in THE STORY

The poetic books do not advance THE STORY in the Old Testament and they fit within the context of the patriarchs (Job) and the kingdom, particularly the lives of David and Solomon (Psalms, Proverbs, Ecclesiastes, and Song of Songs). They deal with everyday life as people sought to live in obedience to the Mosaic Covenant. The books offer reflections concerning a wide variety of topics and provide background to THE STORY told in Genesis, 2 Samuel, and 1 Kings.

Looking Forward to Jesus

Although these books have more to do with reflecting on everyday life in the context of the Mosaic Covenant, the poetic books also advance God's plan. For example, the Psalms are full of references to the Messiah. Consider Psalm 2, 16, 22, 40, 45, 68, 69, 72, 109, 110, and 118. Because of the plethora of passages, we must simply note that the people's anticipation of the one who is coming is rising. The nation awaits the coming of the Messiah and increasingly believes that he is their only hope as earthly systems and people continuously fail.

CHAPTER TWENTY-TWO: THE PROPHETIC BOOKS

The prophetic books do not generally contain stories, although the occasional narrative appears. These books are a collection of sermons, written to reorient a nation's heart to the Lord or to announce judgment on a rebellious nation. As such, they can seem redundant and depressing, full of harsh words and extreme circumstances. However, rightfully understood, these books are a powerful portrayal of both the greatness and the goodness of the Lord.

The prophetic books comprise the last seventeen books of the Old Testament, Isaiah to Malachi. These books are generally divided into the following two broad categories:

MAJOR Prophets: Isaiah, Jeremiah, Lamentations, Ezekiel, and Daniel.

MINOR Prophets: Hosea, Joel, Amos, Obadiah, Jonah, Micah, Nahum, Habakkuk, Zephaniah, Haggai, Zechariah, and Malachi

The Major Prophets are not necessarily "major" because of their size, but rather because they are separate from the Minor Prophets, which were all included on one scroll for fear they would be lost. In the Hebrew Bible, the Minor Prophets are called "The Twelve." Lamentations was also combined onto the Jeremiah scroll with a similar fear that it might be lost.

The prophetic books do not advance THE STORY of the Old Testament. Instead they fit within the time period of 2 Kings through Nehemiah. We do not always know the exact context of each sermon, but each sermon is connected to a real life situation through which the Lord is seeking to work. A good example of this is found in Ezra 5:1 with the mention of Haggai and Zechariah. In Ezra 4:24 we are told that the work on the Temple ceased because of mounting opposition from the people of the land. Those who returned to the land were discouraged, and they lost their tenacious desire to restore the land to a place filled with the worship of the Lord. This is where the sermons of

Haggai fit so clearly. Haggai admonishes them for living in their paneled homes while the Temple was in shambles. He admonished them that their desires to fill their pockets with wealth and live the good life would have devastating consequences. He also reminded them of the greater work the Lord is doing in this world so that it would be filled with his glory. He pleaded with them to join with this work and turn their attention and their wealth back to a proper focus on the Lord. The people responded, and the Temple was quickly completed. This prophetic book makes much more sense when it is seen in its proper historical context, which adds depth and clarifies the sermon's intent. Unfortunately, we do not have this clarity for each prophetic book or sermon, nor does every prophecy even offer the opportunity for a response. However, we need to realize that even if we don't know the specifics there is a story behind every sermon, a story of people living faithlessly while the Lord invites them into relationship with him.

Main Message

So what are the prophets all about? When we come to this section of the Old Testament, the Mosaic covenant is of primary importance. It may be helpful to review the chapter, "Understanding the Covenants," to refresh your memory. The nation entered into covenant relationship at

Mt. Sinai, which brought both privileges and obligations (see Deuteronomy 28; Leviticus 26). When the nation obeyed the stipulations of the covenant, there was blessing. When they disobeyed, they experienced the Law's various curses. The prophets were the Lord's attempts to spare the people of the ultimate judgment—exile. In his mercy, he issued a continual call through the prophets to his people urging them to respond to their responsibilities so they could enjoy the blessings.

This underscores an important aspect of the prophetic message. Many people understand prophecy to be the revelation of something in the future. However, prophecy is less concerned about future events and more concerned with calling the people of the Lord to holy living, whatever that meant in their contemporary situation. It is estimated that less than 5% of the combined prophetic messages concerned the future and less than 1-2% is still future for us today. The focus of the messages was the contemporary situation. Any prophecies concerning the future are only necessary to announce coming judgment if disobedience persists. These future oriented messages also reveal the Lord's unfolding plan of judgment, which will end all evil and usher in his righteous kingdom. Overall, the message is of relationship. The Lord mercifully pursues people so that they can experience life, which is only found in relationship with him.

There were multiple titles for prophetic people in the Old Testament: man of God, seer, visionary, diviner, or prophet. The "man of God" was one perceived as possessing special empowerment from the Lord for service. This person often had a message from the Lord. The "seer" was so named because of the extraordinary insight they received from the Lord. In other words, this person could "see" into situations. The "visionary" was named because the individual received special information in the form of visions and dreams. The "diviner" (see also "soothsayer") practiced formal divination, using many methods to determine the will of deity. However, these individuals were legitimately sanctioned in the Old Testament because the practice was essentially pagan. The final name, "prophet," was an outgrowth of the "man of God" found earlier in the Old Testament. When the literary prophets grew in prominence, "prophet" became the common term. He was one who received a message from the Lord, based on the Mosaic Covenant, to apply to a contemporary situation.

"Prophet" was one of the offices of the Old Testament, which had a connection to the Law. The "judges" provided a verdict concerning any misunderstanding or confusion over the Law. They were experts. The "kings" were to rule according to the Law, not departing to the left or the right. They had the power to enforce the Law. The "priests" and "Levites" were the teachers of the Law. It was their responsibility to engage the people in learning what it meant to live under the Mosaic Covenant. The prophets were concerned with applying the Law in a contemporary situation where obedience was lacking. They challenged people who had grown numb or were simply oblivious to the Law.

Israel struggles throughout her history with rebellion, turning after other gods, and forsaking the goodness of the Lord. Time and time again she finds herself in this situation. So the Lord sends prophets to remind them of their covenant with him. They are spokespersons for God delivering formal messages from the theocratic king, as through a pronouncement, or informal messages, as when someone seeks them out for a word from the Lord. There were even prophetic centers where people could inquire of the Lord through a prophet. And because leadership is integral to the life of Israel, prophetic messages are often directed toward the leadership and contain political overtones. The focus, however, is always the breaking of covenant. Prophecy was not delivered to satisfy curiosity about the future. It was meant to have a practical effect on people's lives and bring greater awareness of holiness through repentance.

In the Old Testament, we find non-literary prophets,

literary prophets, and false prophets. Non-literary prophets are prophets whose messages from the Lord have not been preserved in books that carry their name. Many of these could also be called "pre-literary prophets" because they prophesied before the preservation of prophetic sermons in book form. Some of their sermons are recorded in the books of Samuel, Kings, or Chronicles. Elijah and Elisha are great examples of non-literary prophets who had powerful ministries for the Lord and greatly influenced the nation. Literary prophets are those whose words have been preserved in written form, and these messages still speak to us today. These first two categories of prophets often experienced great difficulty in representing the Lord. Their message was not always well-received and the Lord often had them engage in abnormal behavior to make a point. They were imprisoned, hated, and often misunderstood.

The final category, "false prophets," is so named because these prophets were not of the Lord. They spoke in the names of other gods or they misspoke in the name of the Lord. Their message was deceptive and self-seeking. False prophets created difficulty for the Lord's people and confused them. To help the people deal with any confusion, the Law set forth guidelines in Deuteronomy 18:9-22, outlining true prophesy. Israel was given a helpful responsibility. They were to test what the prophet said to see if it came true (then a prophet would gain a reputation) and to verify the signs of a prophet (signs given by the Lord).

There were five components to the prophetic message. First, there was a statement of God's legal suit against his people. They had broken the covenant, and this was clearly revealed to them. Second, there was an announcement of judgment, which was always given in hope of turning Israel's heart back to the Lord. God's discipline is always merciful at its core. Third, the prophet issued a call to repentance. The Lord knows the human heart's tendency toward sin, so he offers a way back to him. He opens his arms and asks his people to come back. Fourth, the prophets made it clear that Israel's rebellion was not going to stop God's purposes in this world. So the prophet clearly affirmed the good news of God's mercy in spite of Israel's disobedience. And finally, the prophet affirmed God's faithfulness to his covenantal commitment to usher in his kingdom and fulfill his promises. Each prophetic message contained most or all of these components with the whole purpose being to call the Lord's people back into relationship with him.

Their message concerned four situations, and one of the great difficulties of understanding prophecy is determining which situation a particular prophecy is addressing. Consider the following possibilities:

1) the immediate contemporary situation of the people;

2) often with a focus on future captivity or restoration;

3) and many times, there are references to Christ and his kingdom;

4) as well as the ultimate focus, which is the "new heavens and the new earth."

These four situations are often understood to be mountain peaks lined up in a row with only the first one visible; this is prophets' primary focus. The constant focus is the contemporary situation with a call to repent of present rebellion and return to covenant faithfulness. So, when interpreting the prophets, your methodology should always begin with the immediate situation and only move to the "mountain peaks" behind when the text forces you to. That is the safest, most responsible way to understand the prophetic message. Ultimately, prophecy is God's message to the present (immediate situation) in light of his ongoing redemptive purposes and plan for humanity (the other three situations).

Context in THE STORY

So the prophetic books do not advance THE STORY of the Old Testament. Instead, they fit into THE STORY as told in other books. But where exactly is that? The answer, in short, is that they are pre-exilic (prophesying before the exile), exilic (prophesying during the exile), or post-exilic (prophesying after the exile). For a more precise answer, consider the following:

DATE	PROPHET	REIGNING KING(S)	BIBLE NARRATIVE
PRE-EXILE	Obadiah	Jehoram	2 Kings 8-12
	Joel	Joash	2 Kings 11-12
	Jonah	Jereboam II	2 Kings 14
	Amos	Jeroboam II	2 Kings 14
	Hosea	Uzziah, Jotham, Ahaz, and Hezekiah	2 Kings 15-20
	Micah	Jotham, Ahaz, and Hezekiah	2 Kings 15-20
	Isaiah	Uzziah, Jotham, Ahaz, and Hezekiah	2 Kings 15-20
	Nahum	Manasseh and Josiah	2 Kings 21-23
	Zephaniah	Josiah	2 Kings 22-23
	Habakkuk	Josiah	2 Kings 22-24

	Jeremiah	Josiah, Jehoiakim, and Zedekiah	2 Kings 22-25
EXILE	Lamentations	The death of King Josiah	2 Kings 24-25
	Daniel	Jehoiakim – Cyrus	2 Kings 24-Ezra 1
	Ezekiel	Jehoiakim, Zedekiah	2 Kings 24-Ezra 1
POST-EXILE	Haggai		Ezra 5-6
	Zechariah		Ezra 5-6
	Malachi		Nehemiah 13

It is difficult to date each prophetic book precisely as there is a lot of debate whenever a reigning king is not clearly identified. Some of the books also cross the boundaries in the chart above in relation to the exile. However, this chart provides a general idea of how to place the prophetic books within a historical context. Context always helps us better understand the message. The prophets must be read with a general understanding of THE STORY found in 2 Kings through Nehemiah. As you read these books, try to read them alongside the brief history provided in the corresponding chapters.

Looking Forward to Jesus

The prophetic books increasingly draw attention to the coming Messiah. Consider the numerous references to him in the prophets (Joel 2:23; Isaiah 4:2; 7:14; 9:1-7; 11:1-16; 24:21-25; 28:16; 30:19-26; 42:1-7; 49:1-6; 50:4-9; 52:13 – 53:12; 55:3-5; 61:1-3; 63:1-6; Hosea 3:4-5; Amos 9:11-15; Micah 2:12-13; 5:1-4; Jeremiah 23:5-6; 30:9, 21; 33:14-16; Ezekiel 17:22-24; 21:25-27; 34:23-31; 37:15-28; Daniel 7:13-14; 9:24-27; Haggai 2:6-9; 2:21-23; Zechariah 3:8-10; 6:9-15; 9:9-10; 10:4; 11:4-14; 12:10; 13:7; and Malachi 3:1; 4:2). Little by little, the Lord reveals his plan to redeem sinful people and usher in a new kingdom. This increased attention on the Messiah is a result of the nation's growing failure to realize the promises of their covenants with the Lord. The Lord is going to have to do something beyond human means to accomplish his purposes; consequently, the people begin to look forward to that coming day.

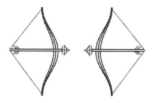

CHAPTER TWENTY-THREE
EXILE

THE STORY of the Old Testament is put on hold for 70 years as the nation of Judah goes into exile. These are sad days for the nation. They have deteriorated to such a degree that the Lord has no other option but to give them the ultimate punishment. The nation was repeatedly warned of future consequences if they did not turn from their wicked ways, but they persisted in their disobedience, feeling justified in the way they were living.

Israel is warned of the consequences for disobedience from the very beginning. Following a listing of laws instructing the Israelites to abstain from engaging in the abominable practices of the Canaanites, who they were to destroy as they took the Promised Land, Leviticus 18:24-30 reads,

Do not make yourselves unclean by any of these things, for by all these the nations I am driving out before you have become unclean, and the land became unclean, so that I punished its iniquity, and the land vomited out its inhabitants. But you shall keep my statutes and my rules and do none of these abominations, either the native or the stranger who sojourns among you (for the people of the land, who were before you, did all of these abominations, so that the land became unclean), lest the land vomit you out when you make it unclean, as it vomited out the nation that was before you. For everyone who does any of these abominations, the persons who do them shall be cut off from among their people. So keep my charge never to practice any of these abominable customs that were practiced before you, and never to make yourselves unclean by them: I am the LORD your God.

Using the terminology of this passage, the consequence of exile meant that the nation had made the land "unclean" with their behavior, so the land "vomited" them out. Later in Leviticus 26, the blessings and curses of the covenant are presented to the people (see also Deuteronomy 28). In verses 14 and following, the Lord reveals the consequences for disobeying him. In these verses, the Lord's discipline intensifies in the face of continued rebellion and hardness of heart until it culminates with a warning of exile in verses 27-33:

> But if in spite of this you will not listen to me, but walk contrary to me, then I will walk contrary to you in fury, and I myself will discipline you sevenfold for your sins. You shall eat the flesh of your sons, and you shall eat the flesh of your daughters. And I will destroy your high places and cut down your incense altars and cast your dead bodies upon the dead bodies of your idols, and my soul will abhor you. And I will lay your cities waste and will make your sanctuaries desolate, and I will not smell your pleasing aromas. And I myself will devastate the land, so that your enemies who settle in it shall be appalled at it. And I will scatter you among the nations, and I will unsheathe the sword after you, and your land shall be a desolation, and your cities shall be a waste.

The prophetic books provided further warnings as many prophets were sent with clear warnings to the people. Israel did not listen and ultimately received the just consequence of exile into a foreign land.

Despite Israel's unfaithfulness, the Lord made it clear that he would continue to be faithful to them. As we continue reading in Leviticus 26:44-45, the Lord confirms his faithfulness: "Yet for all that, when they are in the land of their enemies, I will not spurn them, neither will I abhor them so as to destroy them utterly and break my covenant with them, for I am the LORD their God. But I will for their sake remember the covenant with their forefathers, whom I brought out of the land of Egypt in the sight of the nations, that I might be their God: I am the LORD." This promise underscores the Lord's endless loving-kindness. He is amazing!

Not only did the Lord make this promise, he even foretold the length of the exile: seventy years. Listen to the grace of the Lord:

> "This whole land shall become a ruin and a waste, and these nations shall serve the king of Babylon seventy years. Then after seventy years are completed, I will punish the king of Babylon and that nation, the land of the Chaldeans, for their iniquity, declares the Lord, making the land an everlasting waste" (Jeremiah 25:11-12).

> "For thus says the Lord: When seventy years are completed for Babylon, I will visit you, and I will fulfill to you my promise and bring you back to this place" (Jeremiah 29:10).

Eventually Daniel, while he is in exile in Babylon, studies God's revelation and discovers this precious truth. In Daniel 9:2, he writes, "...in the first year of his reign, I, Daniel, perceived in the books the number of years that, according to the word of the LORD to Jeremiah the prophet, must pass before the end of the desolations of Jerusalem, namely, seventy years." This led to an amazing prayer, where Daniel acknowledges the sin of the nation and pleads for the mercy of the Lord. The end of his prayer, verses 15-19, captures the beauty and humility of his heart:

And now, O Lord our God, who brought your people out of the land of Egypt with a mighty hand, and have made a name for yourself, as at this day, we have sinned, we have done wickedly. O Lord, according to all your righteous acts, let your anger and your wrath turn away from your city Jerusalem, your holy hill, because for our sins, and for the iniquities of our fathers, Jerusalem and your people have become a byword among all who are around us. Now therefore, O our God, listen to the prayer of your servant and to his pleas for mercy, and for your own sake, O Lord, make your face to shine upon your sanctuary, which is desolate. O my God, incline your ear and hear. Open your eyes and see our desolations, and the city that is called by your name. For we do not present our pleas before you because of our righteousness, but because of your great mercy. O Lord, hear; O Lord, forgive. O Lord, pay attention and act. Delay not, for your own sake, O my God, because your city and your people are called by your name.

Daniel

He humbly acknowledges their sin, but pleads for the mercy of the Lord. And the Lord answers. He restores his people back into the land.

The focus of Ezra and Nehemiah is on the three returns from exile. Before you read those books, you must grasp how amazing it is that the Lord would respond in such mercy and that the people would return to the land. It is amazing that the Lord continues to love and pursue his people, making a way for them to have relationship with him. Yet he does. It is amazing that the people will uproot their families from the life they have known for 70 years and return to a land that has been destroyed and will only be restored through great difficulty. If we use Daniel as an example, we know that he had risen to a very powerful position while in exile. He had firmly planted himself in this new country. If he had a family, then this is the only country his children or grandchildren would have known. In other words, the people had settled down and had a new home. Yet they return.

Ultimately, this is all part of God's eternal plan. The northern kingdom went into exile, but we really never hear from them again. The southern kingdom goes into exile, and yet they return. Why? God is not finished with his people. He must get this people back to the land. The Messiah will come from Judah. The Messiah will be born in Bethlehem. God has preserved the Messianic kingly line as well. The Messiah will be born a king. God is on the move. He is making a way. He will fulfill his promises.

The focus here is not just Israel and his promises to them; the Lord is preparing the context to send the good news of the gospel to the world, and the first step is to get the people back into the land. The books of Ezra and Nehemiah provide the story, but nothing extraordinary happens in these books. Everything in these books is preparation. After this story is told, there will 400 silent years. Everything will be in place...waiting...waiting for the biggest event this world will ever know. This event will be the central event of all history. The Messiah will come, God in the flesh. He will die for the sins of the world, be raised from the dead, commission his followers to be ambassadors of his kingdom, and ascend back to heaven. Then he will come again to usher in his kingdom.

The exile shows us that the Lord is slowly advancing his plans. Nothing will stop him. Israel's sins will not stop him. Big, bad, powerful Babylon will not stop him. The next world power, Persia, will not stop him. The difficulties the people experience when they return to the land will not stop him. The 400 silent years will not stop him. He *will* make a way.

CHAPTER TWENTY-FOUR
EZRA/NEHEMIAH

After the 70-year exile, the beginning of which is found at the end of 2 Kings, THE STORY picks up when the people return to the land. There are three returns, and their history is found in Ezra and Nehemiah. Ezra records the events of the first two returns, and Nehemiah records the events of the third return. At the end of these two books, THE STORY of the Old Testament ends.

The title of each book is derived from the name of story's primary character of the story. The use of first person narrative in the book of Ezra (7:28 – 9:15) suggests that Ezra authored the book. Also, Nehemiah 1:1 calls that book, "the words of Nehemiah," which indicates that Nehemiah authored his book as well. However, a separate author may have compiled both books since there is continuity to the narratives. This is further supported by two points. First, in the Hebrew Bible, the books were combined into one. Other translations of the Hebrew documents also unite the books. Second, the closing verses of 1 and 2 Chronicles are the same as the opening verses of Ezra. This allows for an intentional connection between Ezra and Nehemiah, with 1 and 2 Chronicles serving as the background. It is probable that one author compiled all four books to accurately portray the events surrounding the return to the land with a theological emphasis encouraging the people to covenant faithfulness.

The unity is also supported by the similar focus of the Ezra and Nehmiah's lives. They are both reformers of the post-exilic period who encounter, confront, and lead the people through repentance from covenant unfaithfulness. They also have complementary ministries. Ezra, as a priest, is focused on issues surrounding the temple and proper worship. He is probably best remembered for the reading of the law before the people, a story which is actually recorded in the book of Nehemiah (chapter 8). Nehemiah is more "blue collar," focusing on building a wall to protect the capital city of Jerusalem, signifying stability for the nation. He is best remembered for his proactive and comprehensive plan to rebuild the walls while fighting off the enemy. And, finally, they both held political offices in the Persian royal leadership. Ezra was like a secretary for Jewish affairs as a part of the Persian king's royal cabinet (Ezra 7:14, 25). Nehemiah was a cupbearer to the king (Nehemiah 1:11; 2:1).

The two books together demonstrate that Israel has not recovered from her propensity to wander from covenant faithfulness. They underscore the necessity of the Lord's work to accomplish his purposes with his people and fulfill his promises. As such, these books bring the Old Testament to a close and heighten the anticipation for the New Testament and the marvelous work the Lord will do through the Messiah.

Major Divisions

Since the two books record the events occurring after the exile, it is natural to view them as a unit. The overall focus is on the three returns to the land, so it is no surprise that the structure of the book includes such a focus. The structure is as follows:

I.	Ezra 1-6	First Return
II.	Ezra 7-10	Second Return
III.	Nehemiah 1-13	Third Return

Although this outline focuses on the concept of "return," the contents are less about the actual return and more about what happens after them. In each return, Israel makes important advancements as she seeks to restore the land to a place of prominence.

Main Message

The message of these books is an account of the three returns to Israel to rebuild the Temple and the walls of Jerusalem so the people can live in security, restore their exclusive worship of Yahweh, and live in light of the covenant. Seventy years have passed since Babylon took them into exile. A whole generation has lived in a foreign land. They talk like Babylonians (i.e., speak Aramaic) and in many ways have a similar worldview. Jeremiah had prophesied that the time of exile would be 70 years, another reminder that God is clearly working out his purposes in this world and that he is in control of all things. This 70-year time period has passed, so now the people return to the land.

Rarely would a world power, which had invested so much in conquering a nation and had brought them into exile, have a change of heart and say, "Go back to your land." What happened? Theologically, the Lord has completed his people's punishment so he brings them back to their land because he is continuing his work. However, politically, there is a change in world power. The book of Daniel provides the details of this shift. In

Daniel 1:1, Nebuchadnezzar, king of Babylon, is at the height of his reign, the top ruler in the world (see 2 Kings 25). As this powerful nation conquered the world, Israel became one of its many conquests. As the story in the book of Daniel continues, the Lord brings judgment on Babylon, they are conquered, and this brings the shift in power. In Daniel 10:1, Cyrus, king of Persia, is now the world leader as Persia has conquered the Babylonians to take control (see Ezra 1:1). This transfer of power created the opportunity for Israel to return. Persia had no vested interest in this particular people group, so they readily offered them the opportunity. As a result, Israel returns and THE STORY continues.

So why is it important to see both the theological and political reason for their exile's end? Because we need to see how the Lord works through seemingly "natural" events to accomplish his purposes. The "natural" events of nations rising in power and conquering other nations are a phenomenon we see throughout history. The power and prestige the USA enjoys as a nation has only been brief when you consider world history, and both will more than likely have an end, as another nation rises to prominence in her place. Kingdoms rise, and kingdoms fall. However "natural" this may seem, this story enables us to look beyond the seemingly "natural" events and see the greater work of the Lord. It teaches us that we are to understand all events as the intentional and sovereign work of the Lord. Nothing occurs apart from him. You may explain an event as "natural," but the Lord is always supernaturally working to advance his purposes.

There are many intentional connections between the pre-exilic nation and the post-exilic events. Now that the 70 years have passed and the consequences of the exile have been fulfilled, there is an undoing of the destruction Israel experienced. In the latter part of 2 Kings 25, which records Israel's overthrow by the Babylonians, the common theme is destruction. As we enter into the post-exilic events in Ezra and Nehemiah, which records Israel's rebuilding of her land, the common theme is restoration. Consider the following:

2 Kings: Destruction	Ezra-Nehemiah: *Restoration*
2 Kings 24:13 – treasures taken from the Temple	Ezra 1:6 – money given Ezra 6:8 – more money given Ezra 7:15-10 – more money given
2 Kings 24:14 – people taken, except the poor	Ezra 1:1 – 1st return Ezra 7:1 – 2nd return Nehemiah 1:1 – 3rd return

2 Kings 25:9 – the Temple and every house is burned and destroyed	Ezra 3:2 – altar restored Ezra 3:8 – began rebuilding the Temple (completed in 5:1-15; 6:13-15)
2 Kings 25:10 – broke down the walls of Jerusalem	Nehemiah 6:15 – walls of Jerusalem are repaired
2 Kings 25:13-17 – Temple utensils are taken	Ezra 1:7-11 – Temple utensils are returned (cf. 7:19)

The Lord is continuing his work. It will not be stopped. His people rebelled, and they experienced the consequences. But the Lord is not finished with his people. He begins restoring them. Ezra and Nehemiah provide only the beginning of this restoration. The focus is going to change. It is no longer about restoring Israel to a place of prominence in the world. It shifts to something bigger. The Messiah is going to come. Instead of ushering in his kingdom, he is going to suffer and die, the ultimate atoning sacrifice. This part of the Lord's plan is veiled to the nation. They want a kingdom, but they fail to realize that the path to that kingdom is through the atonement provided by the Messiah. He is the way, the truth, and the life. No one comes to the Father but through him (John 14:6). Nonetheless, the nation rebounds ever so slightly. They are back in the land, and restoration is initiated.

The record of the three returns details the restoration and people's continued struggles. Even though Israel has a heightened sense of obedience because they long for the blessing of the Lord, their struggles with obedience are many. In fact, their struggles are similar to what they have experienced throughout their history. The idolatry that resulted from their failure to completely conquer the people of the land is not the issue so much as their failure to keep the Torah central is. There is a cycle that repeats in each return. They begin with a desire to follow the Lord wholeheartedly, which is followed by walking away from the Torah in a significant way, before concluding with the Lord mercifully calling them back to obedience through a prophetic word. The significant difference between the pre-exilic people and the post-exilic people is a new found ability to own their sin and repent. Every time there is a confrontation, it is followed by repentance. The people struggle with their sinful practices, but they increasingly respond with repentance to the mercy of the Lord. Because of this, the events in these books represent some of Israel's better days. In some ways, it is as good as it gets for Israel. This reality underscores the need for a Messiah. How can they ever keep the Law so they can live in the Lord's blessing? They cannot. The wrath they deserve for their continued rebellion must be poured out, and it must be poured out on the Messiah, who will stand as a perfect sacrifice. If this is as good as it gets for Israel, then what they really need is a Savior. The Lord will make a way.

As is often the case in reading the narratives of the Bible, it is unclear to the casual reader how much time takes place in between the returns. They are simply presented as events that follow one another. In some ways it would be helpful if the contents were divided into three obvious sections, with each section containing the story of one return. However, that is not the case.

Each return advances the Lord's purposes. Each return demonstrates the sovereignty of the Lord in accomplishing his purposes. But each return emphasizes the people's struggles to faithfully follow him. Despite their struggles, the Lord mercifully pursues his people and continues to unfold his remarkable plan to redeem a people for his kingdom.

The writing of these books is motivated by theological interests, especially regarding the religious aspects of Israel's life. The focus is on rebuilding the religious capital of the nation, where worship was to be centralized (see Deuteronomy 12). The city of Jerusalem needed to become safe and vibrant so that worship could be uninhibited. The Temple also needed to be rebuilt so the people could worship the Lord as the Law prescribed. During this time the Law is properly emphasized by the people. They seem to understand that they must demonstrate proper obedience to the Lord if they are going to enjoy the blessings of being his people. The time of exile appears to have produced a spiritual hunger in them. They do not want to return to exile as a result of further disobedience. The Torah is to be their guide for life, and they are committing themselves to its teachings. On several occasions, the people are called to repent and change their behavior because they are the people of the Lord and their daily lives are to demonstrate this. They must look like the people of the Lord. As they are called to repent, they respond with hearts that truly want to please the Lord. Additionally, the priestly functions and sacrifices are restored so the people can bring their gifts to the Lord and atone for their sin. Each of these developments makes it clear that the Lord is not finished with his people. He is pursuing them, wooing them back into relationship. He is on the move, and his people will be a part of his plans for this world.

1 and 2 Chronicles

These books do not advance THE STORY. For many readers of the Old Testament, 1 and 2 Chronicles seem unnecessary because they repeat stories that have already been told. However, the specific focus to these books makes them very valuable.

Authorship of the books is uncertain. The Jewish

Talmud ascribes it to Ezra and there is much evidence for this. First, the last few verses of 2 Chronicles and the first verses of the book of Ezra are identical and this is not an accident. Some suppose that 1 and 2 Chronicles are intended as the introduction to the book of Ezra. The identical verses, then, indicate that Ezra now picks up the story. Second, although 1 and 2 Chronicles are a historical record, the focus of the books is on religious history. This necessitates a familiarity with the nation's religious perspective. With his Levitical background, Ezra is a good candidate. Third, those who study literary style have noted similarities between the books that suggest shared authorship. So Ezra probably wrote these books and this is significant.

These books were written to encourage those who had returned. They were entering a land that had been devastated and foes opposed their rebuilding of the nation. They even gave up along the way because of discouragement. The history of 1 and 2 Chronicles gave them reason to persevere. These books demonstrate the Lord's faithfulness to those who have worshipped him as he deserves. The history of the kings highlights those who worshipped the Lord properly and underscores the resulting blessings of the Lord.

How did this encourage the nation? It reminded them why they were doing what they were doing. The task of rebuilding the Temple had enormous ramifications for the nation. The ability to offer sacrifices on the altar and make the land a worship center to the Lord is worth any opposition the people might face. They needed to persevere. They did not want another exile. This was where the Lord chose for his name to dwell and he deserved to be properly worshipped there. And so the people persevered. They worked through their sin. They sought to clean up their lives so the Lord would be glorified and so they could experience his blessings.

These books may seem repetitive, but they were intended to encourage the people. While their actual effect is unknown, we do know that all who pointed the people to faithfulness during this time had a positive impact. God moved. The people responded. Their tasks were accomplished. God was making a way.

Context in THE STORY and Looking Forward to Jesus

THE STORY of the Old Testament comes to an end rather abruptly. Knowing that this is the end of THE STORY is intended to bring a strong reaction of "Nooooooo!!!!" from the reader. In other words, this cannot be the end. What about the multitude of promises recorded throughout the history of Israel? Where is their fulfillment? What about the kingdom? What about the "I will' spoken many times in the prophets concerning what the Lord will do in that "coming day?" What about the "new heavens and the new earth?" What about the coming of the Spirit? And, if we have read closely, what about the suffering servant who would die in their place so they might be redeemed? The questions abound if we have read closely. So, even though THE STORY found in the Old Testament comes to an end, it is clear that this is not *the* end of the larger story. There is more, and that "more" will be found in the New Testament. With this in mind, it may be best to name the Old Testament the "First Testament," which is followed by the "Second Testament," or the "Promise Testament," which is followed by the "Fulfillment Testament." The Lord is not finished with his people or his plans. There is more. Blessed be the name of the Lord!

CHAPTER TWENTY-FIVE
THEOLOGY OF EZRA/NEHEMIAH

As these books bring THE STORY of the Old Testament to a climax, so does their theology bring Old Testament theology to a climax. Nehemiah 9, especially verse 33, crystallizes what we have been reading through THE STORY. The theology is this: The Lord is just and merciful in all his dealings with his people, and, even with the many good attempts at faithfully following the Law, his people run from the Lord's loving pursuit, resulting in rebellion. Nehemiah 9:33 reads, "Yet you have been righteous in all that has come upon us, for you have dealt faithfully and we have acted wickedly." Nehemiah 9 contains a prayer from the Lord's people that focuses on a repeated cycle of the goodness of the Lord and the rebellion of his people. This cycle is bookended by an emphasis on the greatness of the Lord. The first bookend simply acknowledges the Lord's greatness. He is the Creator of all things, and he is to be exalted above all and worshipped (9:5-6). He is the one who keeps the covenant in his loving-kindness (9:32-37). The second bookend acknowledges the people's need to yield to the Lord's greatness. Because he is who he is, his people are to yield their very lives to him in all things, without question. He is to be acknowledged as the supreme sovereign of the universe. Although Israel has done a poor job of this throughout her history, now, as a result of the Lord's good work in them, they to make this commitment.

In this summary of the history of Israel, depicted in the chart above, we see the continuous evidence of Israel's faithlessness and the Lord's faithfulness. Israel is rebellious, and the Lord exhibits goodness. This basically sums up Israel's existence. It is fascinating to note that the cycle begins with the goodness of the Lord and ends with the goodness of the Lord. We must get this, especially in the covenants. The Lord is making a way. His work will be accomplished despite humanity's sinfulness. His goodness is overwhelming. Throughout the chapter you can find references to Israel's history, which can be clearly identified in the biblical text. Consider the following:

Summary	Story in the Old Testament
9:7-8	Genesis 12-50
9:9-20	Exodus – Leviticus
9:21-25	Numbers – Joshua
9:26-31	Judges – 2 Kings
9:32-37	Period of the Exile, Ezra - Nehemiah

This prayer in Nehemiah 9 provides a basic outline of Israel's history.

The Lord's goodness is heightened when we read the warnings of Leviticus 26 which spell out the blessings and the curses of the covenant. The blessings are poured out on the Israelites when they obediently follow the Lord (26:1-13), and the curses are unavoidable when they disobey (26:14-39). The warning of this chapter begins with verses 14-15, "But if you will not listen to me and will not do all these commandments, if you spurn my statutes, and if your soul abhors my rules, so that you will not do all my commandments, but break my covenant, then I will do this to you...." The Lord then outlines his intended response to disobedience. If the nation should continue to turn away in spite of the discipline of the Lord, the Lord will slowly intensify his response. In other words, he will do whatever it takes to get their attention. So, after he sets forth his initial response to Israel's sin, he continues his warning in verse 18, "And if in spite of this you will not listen to me, then I will discipline you again sevenfold for your sins...."

Then again, after he sets forth this heightened response as a result of their continued disobedience, he adds further warning in verse 21, "Then if you walk contrary to me and will not listen to me, I will continue striking you, sevenfold for your sins." And still further consequences are given if they continue in their disobedience as stated in verse 23, "And if by this discipline you are not turned to me but walk contrary to me, then I also will walk contrary to you, and I myself will strike you sevenfold for your sins." And if that were not enough, after more consequences, the Lord adds one more warning in verse 27 if disobedience were to persist, "But if in spite of this you will not listen to me, but walk contrary to me, then I will walk contrary to you in fury, and I myself will discipline you sevenfold for your sins." This last warning will result in exile into foreign lands. It is intended to be the "last straw" for the Lord. Unfortunately for Israel, as they pray this prayer, they are actually experiencing this exact discipline from the Lord (Nehemiah 9:30).

However, fortunately for Israel, in spite of her repeated disobedience, the Lord is merciful. His goodness is repeated throughout Israel's history (9:7-15, 17b, 19-25,

27b, 28b-29a, 30a, and 31). The Lord's goodness is evident in two ways. First, in his provision for Israel he gives them blessings in life (9:7-15, 19-25, and 30a). These blessings range from his gracious provisions to sending them prophets to warn them of their rebellion. He has proven himself to be a loving father to them, anticipating and providing for their every need. Second, the Lord responds in compassion to Israel's sins. Listen to the common theme in these verses:

9:17b   "But you are a God ready to forgive, gracious and merciful, slow to anger and abounding in steadfast love, and did not forsake them."

9:27b   "And in the time of their suffering they cried out to you and you heard them from heaven, and according to your great mercies you gave them saviors who saved them from the hand of their enemies."

9:31   "Nevertheless, in your great mercies you did not make an end of them or forsake them, for you are a gracious and merciful God."

What is the commonality in the Lord's response throughout Israel's history? "Great mercies." The great mercies of the Lord are always available to Israel and to anyone who humbly acknowledges his majesty and bows to his sovereignty in repentance. Listen to Leviticus 26:40-41, "But if they confess their iniquity and the iniquity of their fathers in their treachery that they committed against me, and also in walking contrary to me, so that I walked contrary to them and brought them into the land of their enemies—if then their uncircumcised heart is humbled and they make amends for their iniquity, then I will remember my covenant...." No questions asked. The Lord will be faithful and restore his people, bringing them back under the blessings of the covenant. This is great compassion, undeserved and irresistible.

This brings us to a very important theological point that has been demonstrated throughout Israel's history and is reinforced in the gospel. We come to the Lord, not on our own merit, but according to his mercy. Ephesians 2:8-9 says, "For by grace you have been saved through faith. And this is not your own doing; it is the gift of God, not a result of works, so that no one may boast." This is not just New Testament teaching. It is who the Lord is, and the Old Testament reinforces this. When the Lord says, "I am the Lord," he is claiming both his greatness *and* his goodness. Consider the basic theology for coming to the Lord:

Humanity is sinful. Sin is inescapable this side of heaven. All are under sin. All sin. All will sin until that day when the Lord ushers in his kingdom in its fullness. No one can say, "I have not sinned."

The proper response to God is not, "I must get it all together and come before you sinless. I will give you reason to be good to me." The proper response to God is, "I come to you humbly, seeking your mercy and forgiveness for my sin. Help me."

He knows our frailty, and he responds to our humility with mercy. When a person comes before him and requests forgiveness, he freely grants pardon. He alone can deal with our sin (through the shedding of blood and ultimately in Jesus), and he has promised to do so.

In light of the atonement he offers those who seek his mercy, those who do receive his mercy will subsequently respond, "Because your loving-kindness is great and your mercies are new every morning, I will dedicate myself to live for you and your glory above all things." The response of gratitude will be to exalt the one who alone is able to save.

In other words, the purpose of the Lord's loving-kindness is to incline hearts to him, to worship him and live for his glory. So, throughout Israel's history, the Lord's mercy in response to Israel's rebellion was to woo them into relationship with him. Why would they go anywhere else? For us, it is the same. Our inclination to sin makes it clear that there is nothing we can do to earn his favor. As we humbly come before him, the grace he offers is unbelievable. Because of his abundant offer of grace, we have nothing to prove and nothing to lose. We can, therefore love him and live for him without fear. Thus, when we sin again, which we will do, we turn to him again for mercy, and his mercy is available. Our gratitude for his mercy should abound, leading to a depth of love which is demonstrated by a growing faithfulness to the Lord's purposes. We become one with him as we live in this world. All things become for his glory and are directed toward his purposes. This is the only place where life is found and that is why the Lord repeatedly calls his people to live in this way. This is really good "good news." To him be the glory, great things he has done.

Making It Real

1)   What would it look like if your life history was written out like Israel's in Nehemiah 9? Could you even write a brief history now? In other words, could you recount the ways the Lord has pursued you, poured his love on you, shown mercy, and yet you walked away? Take a moment to rehearse your own history.

2)   The prayer of Nehemiah 9 begins and ends with the greatness of the Lord. At the beginning of the prayer, his greatness is acknowledged, and at the conclusion Nehemiah yields to the Lord's greatness. What is the difference between acknowledging it and submitting to it?

For some, they live as if he is not even God and ignore his greatness. Where are you in life right now: ignoring, acknowledging, or yielding? Pray that the Lord would make your heart one that yields to his greatness.

3)   You may have friends or family who are at different places: ignoring, acknowledging, or yielding. Pray for them. Ask the Lord to continue working in them, making them the kind of people who yield to his greatness.

4)   Thank the Lord for his loving-kindness. Praise his name that he can be so great, yet be so merciful. Give glory to him for the ways he has demonstrated mercy to you time and time again.

CHAPTER TWENTY-SIX
PRELUDE TO THE NEW TESTAMENT

The Old Testament is not intended to be a stand-alone story. It is only a beginning. It demands a sequel. If Nehemiah is the end of THE STORY, then Israel is to be pitied, and we have no hope. There is more to the story.

The rest is found in the New Testament. The Old Testament is a prelude to the New. Everything in the Old Testament points forward to something better in the New. The book of Hebrews refers to the Old Testament as "copies" or "shadows" of what is come (Hebrews 8:5; 9:23; 10:1; Colossians 2:16-17). There is more, and it is better. It all points to Christ. The point of Hebrews is to help us see that Christ is better. There is no reason to go back to being a Jew as prescribed in the Old Testament. The Old Testament pointed to the "better" of Christ.

It all began in the Garden of Eden. The Lord created a perfect place of peace, rest, and, best of all, relationship with him. We have little idea what life was like in the garden, but we can suppose that with the absence of sin it was a paradise. With Genesis 3 comes sin, which ruined this paradise. Sin damaged both the horizontal (human to human) and vertical relationships (human to God). We see the impact in Adam and Eve as they shift the blame rather than own their sin. They cover themselves, not just physiologically, but relationally too. Self-consciousness brings self-centeredness. We also see the impact on Cain and Abel. Cain murders Abel because the Lord was not pleased with his offering like he was with Abel's. Cain's solution is to get rid of his competition. Soon the impact of sin is seen on the whole world as the Lord quickly brings judgment to all of his creation, except Noah and his family, because of sin's pervasiveness. In other words, the perfect place of peace, rest, and relationship with the Lord is lost. However, hope is offered for its return. Genesis 3:15 hints at the one who is to come, the promised Messiah, who will crush evil and restore the Lord's rest. Until that day, THE STORY of the Old Testament is focused on restoration. The Lord provides salvation for Noah and his family, leaving a faithful remnant. The Lord sets his affection on Abram and calls a people for himself out of all the nations of the world. The Lord perseveres with this nation, blessing them, disciplining them, doing everything he can to draw their hearts to him so they can know the life that comes from him alone. The nation's sin becomes so bad they are taken into exile. After 70 years they return, but they still struggle with sin.

Throughout this time, there are repeated attempts to restore the peace, rest, and relationship with the Lord. However, it is obvious there is a *growing need*. They cannot keep the Law. People are rebellious, and they struggle to acknowledge the Lord's sovereignty. There is also a *growing failure*. Every generation battles sin. It is unavoidable. In the words of Isaiah, there is none who does good; no not one. And there is a *growing focus*. The prophets begin to make it clear that the Lord is going to do something beyond the human capacity to obey. The Lord is going to send one who will take the sins of the world and be punished in their place. The Lord is going to send the Messiah, who will bring redemption to sinful people and usher in the kingdom of the Lord through his death, burial, and resurrection. The hope of a perfect place of peace, rest, and relationship with the Lord now rests with the Messiah. A new covenant is coming, one through which the Lord will pour out his Spirit on humanity and give them a new heart with new passions. This covenant will be available to the world, as the good news will go beyond Israel's borders to the ends of the Earth. The Lord will be honored and worshiped as he deserves. The Lord will make a way for this to happen.

In the Old Testament, this is only a promise, but it is fulfilled in the New Testament. The Old Testament waits in longing, but there is hope. The Lord is going to do something spectacular. All creation, especially Israel, waits for him to move. Even with the coming of Jesus, the people asked, "is this the one or shall we wait for another?" The story of the Old Testament is a prelude to the coming of the Messiah. He is the preeminent one to whom every knee will bow and of whom every tongue will confess that he is Lord. In him sinful, rebellious people will find salvation.

Why do we have the Old Testament if ultimately it is all about Jesus, the Messiah? Hopefully, the answer to this has become clear as we have worked our way through THE STORY. There is much to glean from its pages. We learn about the Lord. We learn about ourselves—sinful, stubborn, unfaithful, and rebellious—everything God is not. We see him in his glory. We see the way he works in people's lives. We see his love and perseverance in the face of sin. We see that redemption comes from him alone and, according to his timing. We see that he is matchless, above all, beyond all, and yet he can be known and wants to be known. We see that he has all power. I could go on.

Studying the Old Testament helps us understand the

New Testament. Without a knowledge of the Old Testament, think of the problems we can have in reading the New Testament:

* *the reactions to Jesus in the gospels can be misunderstood;
* *the struggles in the early church, culminating in the Jerusalem Council, can be confusing;
* *Paul's argument for the gospel in Romans will have gaps if we do not understand the beginning of the Lord's work through Abraham or the purpose of the Mosaic Law;
* *the book of Galatians will be a mystery;
* *the argument of Hebrews will make no sense;
* *Old Testament imagery, which the New Testament uses, will be lost, weakening the New Testament's impact on the reader;
* *discussions of the Law will be lacking;
* *the amazing wonder of the gospel going to the Gentiles will not inspire the wonder it should have;
* *and many more.

I hope you get the point by now. The Old Testament paves the way for the New Testament. It is the soil out of which the promises of the Lord grow. It is rich and necessary for us.

Paul gives us a powerful lesson in 1 Corinthians 10:1-14. The passage begins, "I do not want you to be unaware, brethren,…" Paul sees that our study of the Old Testament is vital. The Lord was working in their midst, but he was not pleased with most of them (10:5). So why read and study all these stories if the Lord was not well pleased with them? Verse 6 says, "Now these things took place as examples for us, that we might not desire evil as they did." Verse 11 reiterates this, "Now these things happened to them as an example, but they were written down for our instruction, on whom the end of the ages has come." They are for our instruction so that in every temptation we will not be idolaters, but rather the kind of people who honor the Lord. When we encounter difficulty, we will not look to created things for deliverance; instead, we will look to the Creator, who alone can offer us life. This ties us back to our theology of Genesis, and then to the theology of Exodus, and so on. These stories have everything to do with our lives. They mentor us and warn us.

The author of Hebrews also provides a glorious perspective on why the Old Testament is prelude. In fact, the point of Hebrews is that the Old Testament points to something better. Consider the argument of Hebrews:

*a better covenant, Hebrews 7:22; 8:6-7, 13
*a better law, Hebrews 7:18-19; 8:10-12

*a better sacrifice, Hebrews 7:27; 9:28; 10:12; cf. 9:6-7, 11-14, (23-28); 10:11-14

*a better access to God, Hebrews 10:19-22; 10:39

This is all possible because Jesus, the promised Messiah of the Old Testament, came. It is not that the Old Testament was bad; rather, it is that the Old Testament was pointing to something better. The message of the Bible is that the Lord is making a way for people to be reconciled to him through Jesus. The Old Testament begins that beautiful message, but it culminates in the spectacular story of the gospel. I hope you never get over the wonder of the gospel and the beauty of God's plan to save.

As good and rich as the Old Testament is, it is only the beginning. It is all a prelude to the most beautiful plan of all time: the Lord saves sinners through the death, burial, and resurrection of Jesus. Amazing! It was so amazing that Israel missed it. But the Lord has promised to do a work in their hearts one day (see Romans 10-11). Until then, praise be to the Lamb who was slain because the gospel is going to the nations. I, for one, am saved because of this glorious plan. I marvel in it. I stand amazed. I am full of wonder. Thanks be to the Lord, who was, and is, and is to come. To him be the glory, both now and forever more. Amen.

APPENDIX

Begin with prayer asking God to teach you as you study. This is the necessary preliminary step to the process. Then, read the Biblical text and complete this worksheet, noting chapters and verses for any answers, based on your reading. Pay close attention to the questions as you read. Noting chapters and verses is essential to this project–do not record any answer without noting chapter/verse. There are five questions to answer:

1) What seems to be the main message of the book? Where do you see this message in the book (i.e., support your answer)?

2) What seem to be the major divisions of the book? Include chapters with each division. (Even if you outline

the book, put the major divisions as an answer to this question)

3) What are some of the major topics discussed and what does the book teach about each? This would be topics that the book seems to focus on. Note the topic and what you learn about each one.

4) What questions do you have about the book's contents? What do you not understand? Note the answers you find as you read.

5) What are some applications for your life or the church in general? (Be reflective and note chapters/verses)

The ultimate goal of this project is to develop a better understanding of the book by analyzing each section and sub-section and synthesizing the relationships between the sections in order to identify possible themes. It should be your own work with no helps (such as study Bibles)! For every book containing 10+ chapters, it may be time consuming to divide by paragraph, and you might choose to do only chapters. If so, begin with step #4.

> Step #1   Use a Bible that shows paragraph divisions. Write the verses corresponding to each paragraph down the side of the page with each chapter clearly differentiated.
>
> Step #2   Read each paragraph and briefly

summarize the contents into a thematic statement (one word or a phrase).

Step #3   Note the relationships between the paragraphs and then group related paragraphs into a section (a section may be a whole chapter). Briefly summarize the section into a thematic statement.

Step #4   Briefly summarize the contents of each chapter into a thematic statement.

Step #5   If necessary, group related chapters and briefly summarize these larger sections into a thematic statement.

Step #6   Observe the themes which have emerged, especially from the larger sections, and formulate an overall theme for the book.

Here is an example of outlining from paragraphs:

Paragraphs	Larger Sections	Chapters	
vv 1-5	Day One		
vv 6-8	Day Two	Sustaining	
vv 9-13	Day Three	Environment	
vv 14-19	Day Four		Days of Creation
vv 20-23	Day Five	Living	
vv 24-31	Day Six	Beings	

**related chapters can be grouped to form larger sections.

SPECIAL THANKS

There are many who have contributed to the writing of this book. I first studied the Bible under the pastoral ministry of my Dad and the ministry of my parents, Drs. John and Bette Talley, in our home. When I entered college, my first Old Testament course was taught by Dr. Rick Fairman at Southeastern Bible College. I made a "C" in this course. However, it was when I entered seminary at Grace Theological Seminary that I grew to love the Old Testament under the mentorship of Dr. Richard Averbeck while I studied for and earned my ThM in Old Testament. I continued my PhD work in Theological Studies with an emphasis on the Old Testament under his mentorship at Trinity Evangelical Divinity School. I owe a debt of gratitude to Dr. Averbeck. I would not even be certain what is his in the pages that follow because all of my thinking is built on his teaching of the Old Testament. More than his scholarship, his love for God is what marked my life in those early years of seminary.

It was Biola University's Talbot School of Theology which gave me the opportunity to teach. Thanks to Dr. John Hutchison (and the Bible Exposition Department), Dr. Mike Wilkins, and Dr. Dennis Dirks for taking a huge risk on me. The administration at Biola/Talbot has been very generous in being patient with my developing scholarship and in providing time and funds for research leaves and sabbaticals. It is truly a joy to teach at this university.

The Division of Biblical and Theological Studies has been a tremendous encouragement to me, personally, professionally, and financially. This is probably the finest undergraduate biblical and theological studies faculty in the world, maintaining strong commitments to both scholarship and mentorship. Thanks especially to my Department of Old Testament colleagues, Dr. Ron Pierce, Dr. Ed Curtis, Dr. Jeff Volkmer, and Dr. Charlie Trimm. You each have something I wish I had and, therefore, we make a great team.

My previous Teacher/Research Assistant, Adam Day, is also owed my gratitude. He made teaching much easier by offering his assistance to me for many years, and he assumed additional responsibilities of helping me in my research by doing whatever I asked of him. His assistance was invaluable to me, and his contributions are found in the pages that follow. He was one of the many students who have sharpened my thinking and shaped my own heart over the years. My students at Biola have been incredible to me. I have learned more about the Old Testament from many of them because of their diligent work. Thanks to all of you.

My personal editor and friend, Charlene Ponzio, must also be thanked. She not only reviewed my grammar and syntax, she also gave much needed input to my communication style and content. She has a good grasp of the message of the Bible and her keen eye and heart added to this book. It was a privilege to have an editor who loves Jesus and wants to make sure any book that is written honors him and his message.

The people of the church where I worship and regularly teach, Grace Evangelical Free Church of La Mirada/Fullerton and La Gracia, are the ones who truly call me to understand the Bible and teach it with clarity. Their patience with me as a teacher of God's word and their relentless pursuit of truth encourage me to do my best work when I stand before them and open God's word. This community of believers has been an amazing catalyst for my growth. The leadership of this church is a constant joy to me as we "do life together." The men who regularly mark my life would be too many to mention, but you know who you are. My life would be empty without you. I love you all dearly as you challenge me to walk with Jesus daily.

My partner in ministry, Dr. Erik Thoennes, has marked my life more than most men and more than he will ever know. His love for Jesus has deepened my love for him. He not only teaches me, he lives what he believes. He and I have been through a lot over the years, and we are committed to stay the course until we die or until Jesus comes. I could never do this alone. We do battle together. I love this friend and faithful partner.

My brother, John, has encouraged me deeply through the years, both by his life and by his words. Many times I felt like I had nothing to offer, and his words brought life to my downcast soul. Oftentimes, he had no idea of the "demons" I was fighting. John, your encouragement has been faithful and timely. Keep it coming.

My dear wife and children have served as my greatest challenges and my greatest joys through the years. I love them so much. Joni is incredible, my best friend, and nothing I do would be possible without her. She has been by my side, supporting me through everything God has brought to us since we wed in 1984. She helps me to live what I teach. My children, Amanda and Andrew, are my greatest teachers of the Bible as they have challenged me to know what I believe and live what I believe. They both have much integrity, so it is not possible to play games with them. They have brought me so much joy.

When it is all said and done, there is but one who deserves thanks, my Lord and Savior, Jesus Christ. I boast in him, his cross, and him alone. I want to know him. To him be the glory both now and forever more.